DATE DUE

JE 22 '93	AP 18 01		
SE 16 '94	OC 27 05		
SE 30 94	NO 19 07		
FE 24 '95			
DE 15 95			
MR 1 96			
AP 19 '96			
AP 7 '97			
OC 17 '97			
AP 23 98			
MR 1 '99			
NO 3 99			
OC 23 00			

PENGUIN BOOKS

TYING THE KNOT

Yona Zeldis McDonough is a graduate of Vassar College and Columbia University. Her fiction and nonfiction have appeared in *Bride's, Cosmopolitan, Family Circle, Harper's Bazaar, Modern Bride, The New York Times, The Village Voice,* and a number of literary magazines. She lives in New York City with her husband.

Certified Social Worker Howard Yahm is co-director of the Center for Family Treatment and Divorce Mediation in Rockland County and New York City. He received a certificate in psychoanalytic psychotherapy from the Institute for Contemporary Psychotherapy and is a fellow of the Society of Clinical Social Work Psychotherapists. Mr. Yahm currently conducts his private practice in New York City and Rockland County, New York.

TYING THE KNOT

A Couple's Guide to

Emotional Well-being

from Engagement to

the Wedding Day

YONA ZELDIS McDONOUGH

with Howard Yahm, CSW

PENGUIN BOOKS

PENGUIN BOOKS
Published by the Penguin Group
Viking Penguin, a division of Penguin Books USA Inc.,
40 West 23rd Street, New York, New York 10010, U.S.A.
Penguin Books Ltd, 27 Wrights Lane,
London W8 5TZ, England
Penguin Books Australia Ltd,
Ringwood, Victoria, Australia
Penguin Books Canada Ltd, 2801 John Street,
Markham, Ontario, Canada L3R 1B4
Penguin Books (N.Z.) Ltd, 182–190 Wairau Road,
Auckland 10, New Zealand

Penguin Books Ltd, Registered Offices:
Harmondsworth, Middlesex, England

First published in Penguin Books 1990

1   3   5   7   9   10   8   6   4   2

Copyright © Yona Zeldis McDonough, 1990
All rights reserved

LIBRARY OF CONGRESS CATALOGING IN PUBLICATION DATA
McDonough, Yona Zeldis.
Tying the knot : a couple's guide to emotional well-being from
engagement to the wedding day / Yona Zeldis McDonough with Howard
Yahm
p.   cm.
ISBN 0 14 01.2021 1
1. Betrothal—United States—Psychological aspects.   I. Yahm,
Howard.   II. Title.
HQ801.M4875   1990
306.81—dc20   89-16311

Printed in the United States of America
Set in ITC Garamond Light
Designed by Liney Li

For My Husband, With Love

◆

Acknowledgments

◆

I wish to thank Kenneth E. Silver for encouraging me to see that my own experience might be of interest—and use—to other people. I also want to thank Howard Yahm, whose clinical experience and perspective have been so important to me. Finally, I am indebted to Marian Young and Mindy Werner for their kind help at various stages along the way.

—Y.Z.M.

Contents

◆

Introduction

♦

When I got engaged five years ago, I was happy beyond my wildest expectations. I was twenty-eight and living with the man I loved, but had already started to wonder whether our relationship would ever be formalized by the time-honored ritual of a wedding. Once we became engaged, I put all that worry behind me: planning the wedding promised to be the most exciting fulfillment of all my romantic fantasies. But to my surprise and—indeed dismay—planning the wedding turned out to be more emotionally draining than I ever would have imagined. For one thing, I had to contend with my parents, who had gone through an especially acrimonious divorce and had not laid eyes on each other since their last vicious courtroom battle. Asking them both to be in the same room and remain civil was no small matter. Added to that were the usual problems about money—my fiancé and I were footing the bill ourselves; time—I had started a new job in a busy public relations department and my fiancé was trying to juggle a demanding schedule teaching photography with high-pressure free-lance work; and a very healthy dose of emotional ambivalence—my fiancé had been married—unhappily—before and was apprehensive about trying again; I wondered about the wisdom of marrying someone several years my senior and of another religion. The months before the wedding—which I had envisioned as a heady, carefree time—were actually a tense and difficult period for both of us. And underlying it all was a sense of having been cheated: Wasn't this supposed to be the happiest time of my life? What was going wrong?

On a busy afternoon in which I had a fitting for my dress, finally found the right shoes, and examined at least thirty different veils and headpieces, I headed into a book store—I was looking for a travel book to get started on the honeymoon plans—and found myself gravitating toward the wedding section. I certainly didn't have an expectation of discovering a book that would solve my particular emotional dilemmas, but I was hoping (perhaps unconsciously) to rekindle what I imagined was the proper spirit for planning a wedding. There was no shortage of selections: The shelves were filled with books on food and flowers, decoration and dresses, etiquette and event planning. Most of these books were lovely to look at and many seemed to be eminently useful. But I began to notice a curious similarity in their underlying message:

If the surface of your wedding—the invitations, the floral arrangements, the meal, the clothes—were perfect; then, by extension, you would have the perfect wedding.

Well, I knew from my own experience that something was missing in this equation and that while I was thoroughly enchanted by all the external trappings of the wedding, I could already see that, in and of themselves, they were not going to insure a flawless wedding day. In fact, I had begun to realize—slowly and with much difficulty—that the whole notion of a flawless wedding was doomed from the start. No person—not my fiancé or myself—was without failings. A relationship was made up of two imperfect and very human beings; the wedding would have to accommodate whatever limitations the particular individuals possessed. Yet I also could see that it was possible to have the wedding I had already dreamed of; I simply had to come down to reality first.

It was these insights that prompted me to write this book. If you are looking for a book to help you plan your wedding according to a neatly organized timetable, tips on the best way to find a caterer or buy a wedding dress, this is not the one for you. But if you want a book that seriously addresses all the complicated feelings that emerge during the engagement period, then look no further.

All too often, the only emotions even discussed in connection with a wedding are the pleasant ones: Centuries of fairy tales, folklore, and myth have created the concept of wedding as bliss and release from life's difficulties. This magic has rubbed off on the engagement as well, which is supposedly the happiest time of your life, filled only with delightful thoughts of heirloom dresses and three-tiered cakes. While it is true that the engagement is a period brimming with fantasy, it is also true that the mythology surrounding marriage has made it nearly impossible to talk about any of the more complex feelings—not all of them good—connected with the event. "Why am I suddenly feeling so distrustful of my fiancé?"; "Why are we arguing over such petty things?"; "How can I possibly deal with my mother's guest list without hurting her feelings?"; and "Is marriage going to be the end of romance?" are questions that may be on your mind right now. "Are my divorced parents going to ruin my wedding day?" was certainly one that I confronted over and over as I tried to plan my own wedding.

Arranged as an emotional blueprint, the chapters in *Tying the Knot* map out the most powerful and most commonly felt emotional states of the engagement period. Although you may not experience all the emotions that are discussed nor will you necessarily experience them in this order, it is likely that you will have most if not all of these feelings at some point during the engagement.

Although my own experience was the impetus for this book, I have interviewed approximately fifty couples—both engaged and recently married—to get a sense of what other people were feeling as they moved through the planning process. There was no problem finding source material—it seemed that everyone had a story of prewedding craziness and was eager to tell it.

In large part, a happy engagement and wedding will depend upon your ability to acknowledge all your feelings during the eventful weeks and months ahead. But acknowledgment is only the first step; managing your feelings is the all-important second phase. *Tying the Knot* offers practical suggestions that will help both you and your fiancé to cope. The more able you are to resolve the complex emotional issues of the engagement, the happier the wedding day—and indeed the marriage—will ultimately be.

Although this book is written first and foremost with the bride in mind, almost everything in it—with a few exceptions—applies equally well to the groom. I hope that you share the insights and observations offered here with your fiancé, as a way of opening up the lines of communication during this all-important time.

Last but not least, *Tying the Knot* was written in consultation with Howard Yahm, psychotherapist and co-founder of the Center for Family Treatment and Divorce Mediation in New York City and Rockland County, New York. Yahm believes that you and your fiancé can use the prewedding period as a potentially rewarding opportunity for growing even closer and learning more about each other. To this end, he has outlined a number of emotional tasks for you to address. These tasks arise out of a concept called the Family Life Cycle, a family-systems theory developed by therapists and authors Betty Carter and Monica McGoldrick. This approach has proved highly successful in understanding many family and relationship problems. According to this theory, all the major events in a family's history, whether positive—like a birth or a marriage—or negative—like a divorce or a death—represent crisis points because of the enormous changes they force you to undergo. Every crisis, says Yahm, provides the chance for either emotional damage or emotional growth. Since getting married is one of these crisis points, Yahm sees it as a potential opportunity for significant emotional growth. But to facilitate that growth you and your fiancé need to focus on:

1. Learning to communicate in clear, need-satisfying, anxiety-reducing ways.

2. Developing skills for solving problems and conflicts.

3. Moving toward greater interdependence with one another and moving away from the more one-sided dependence on your respective parents.

4. Achieving a balance between loyalty and togetherness on the one hand and a healthy separateness and independence on the other.

5. Coming to terms with your respective limitations and the ways in which you each fall short of perfection.

6. Recognizing that you are each in constant flux and that you are both marrying a "moving picture," not a "snapshot." This means that you and your fiancé must adapt to and support that ongoing development and the ever-changing needs of one another.

7. Regulating and learning to coordinate your varying needs for emotional closeness and emotional distance. At different points in the relationship, you will each experience different needs for being close to, and alternatively, withdrawing from each other; learning to tolerate and work out those differences is something that should begin now.

8. Learning to maintain a satisfying sexual bond within a long-term, multifaceted relationship. How do you make the transition into sexuality as you become closer on a whole range of important but decidedly unsexy issues—money, kids, career, home? Sexuality in the context of a dating situation (if you are in fact involved in a premarital sexual relationship) is often easier: There are fewer emotional entanglements that act as an impediment to the expression of your sexual feelings. In other words, you may feel more free to be erotic in a less emotionally encumbered situation. All this changes when you decide to get married, and you will need to integrate all these new roles and expectations into your sex life.

The emotion-focused chapters in *Tying the Knot* are meant to help you in your effort to fulfill these tasks. At various points throughout the book, you will find Yahm's other comments on the subjects under discussion; look for his insights whenever you see this symbol:

—YONA ZELDIS MCDONOUGH

TYING THE KNOT

1.

ELATION:

Let's Get Married

◆

□ *The Magic Words*

I'll never forget the moment my husband, Paul, asked me to marry him. We were strolling through a lush, beautifully tended park in the exquisite Spanish city of Barcelona. Just as the sun was sinking behind a cluster of trees, he stopped by a small bridge and uttered those four small but earth-shaking words: "Will you marry me?" I just nodded, unable at that moment to say more.

And yet, the answer to his question seemed like a foregone conclusion: We had been happily living together for more than a year and had just spent the last few weeks on a lazy, romantic drive through the Spanish countryside. We knew we loved each other and wanted to be together, so the marriage proposal was hardly a surprise for either of us. Instead, it felt like the natural next step in a solid, secure relationship that had already survived its share of emotional highs and lows.

But despite all that, something about those words changed everything. We just stood there for a few minutes, holding hands and looking out over the trees, where the sun had now gone. The air was warm and rosy in the late afternoon light, and suddenly we were so overcome with the sense of elation—we were really going to get married—that we couldn't stop smiling. Hand in hand, we walked to a little outdoor café where we ordered a bottle of wine. We were still too overcome to say much, so we just sipped our wine, quietly celebrating our good fortune in finding ourselves here, across from each other in this lovely spot, toasting the marvelous future on which we were about to embark.

Falling in love is just one kind of magic; the decision to get married, while certainly one of love's natural outgrowths, has a thrill all its own. With this declaration, your relationship has reached its absolute peak in terms of commitment, love, and optimism for a shared future. You are bound to feel like a couple of big-time winners—centuries worth of culture and history are all on your side, telling you in no uncertain terms that you have made the right decision.

Since love has traditionally been sanctified and legitimated by marriage, you have (probably without your even knowing it) become a part of an age-old practice that affirms your decision. What you will notice is the deluge of *approval* that often pours in, not only from family and friends, but from perfect strangers. When my fiancé of fifteen minutes told the waiter in his halting Spanish that we were getting married, the man returned to our table with another bottle of wine, which he insisted was on the house. Suddenly, we noticed glasses being raised in our direction, and several friendly greetings and smiles coming our way. Unknowingly, we had entered into a new, magical realm where all the initiates were waiting to greet us with open arms. "Come on in," they seemed to be saying, "the water's fine!"

You may also find that you are treated differently in other areas of your life once you become engaged. Candace, a twenty-seven-year-old university librarian, had been in the same job for several years when she announced to her colleagues her upcoming marriage. Within the next few months, she had received not only a promotion and a raise, but also an office of her own—something which she had very much wanted but been unable to obtain despite her persistent efforts. "I can't say that these professional changes were the direct result of my getting engaged," she says, "but I could feel that in some way my status with my coworkers was now different. Before, I was the only unmarried woman in a community of older, married people; I knew that they very much saw me as a kind of younger sister or daughter. But once I got engaged, I had joined their ranks and become one of them. I don't think anyone thought about this consciously, but it was uncanny how my professional situation changed so quickly on the heels of my personal one."

Deciding to get married is also a passport to feeling accepted and even, for many people, normal. Now this may
sound just a bit anticlimactic—after all, what's so thrilling
about just being normal? But Becky, a thirty-one-year-old
attorney, describes it this way: "I've always been something of a nonconformist. When I graduated from college,
all my friends were heading straight for professional
schools, but I went to India for a year. I did a lot of
traveling, had relationships with—well—let's just say
some pretty unconventional types, and worked in the
theatre before I finally figured out that I wanted to be a
lawyer. It's not that I had anything against marriage; it
just seemed like it wasn't for me. So when I met Phil, and
eight months later he proposed, there was this thrilled
little voice inside me that said, 'You're not so weird after
all. You can have what other people have.' It felt great!"

Becky is hardly alone in her feelings. Whether you
have believed that you are the "marrying kind" or you
have found it difficult to imagine sharing your life with
another human being, you have now decided—as most
people finally do—to settle down with one other person.
There is often a sense of relief that accompanies such a
decision, and a pleasantly surprised feeling of "Hey, guess
what, it turns out I'm normal after all."

□ *The Keys to Adulthood*

Though, historically, the people who got married weren't
always adults (Shakespeare's Juliet was only fourteen

when her parents tried to arrange a match for her), getting married is nevertheless considered one of the major milestones of adulthood. When you decide to marry, you move away—literally and figuratively—from your parents, to create a new family unit. Part of the typical engagement elation comes from reaching this milestone.

There is a very special sense of adulthood conferred upon you now; you may feel your own emotional power in a new and surprising way. Even women who hold high-level, responsible jobs are not immune from the "Now I'm really grown-up" feeling of elation that comes with the declaration of marriage. Part of this comes from the extended adolescence that many of us experience: what with college, professional school, and the high cost of rents, lots of young women and men are financially tied to their parents until well into their twenties and even early thirties. In this context, getting married seems like one of the more adult choices you are able to make.

□ *The Party of a Lifetime*

Your wedding is probably the single largest party you will ever hold in your life. The opportunity for large-scale ritual celebration has long been on the decline, but happily enough, weddings are a reversion to a time when people really knew how to throw a party.

Before you even begin the actual planning, you are bound to feel elated by the prospect of uniting family and friends for this joyous event. The great friends from the office you've told your parents about, the eccentric but adorable uncle you've regaled your friends with stories of will finally have a chance to meet one another and these meetings will all take place in the context of your own special day.

But there's another, even more literal, way in which your wedding is the party of a lifetime. Because it is such a central event, it gives you the chance to invite people from all states and corners of your life, so that you actually see your life parade before you in the form of your guests. Grade school chums can rub shoulders with college roommates; long-lost cousins converse with your pals from the health club. Every aspect of your life—family, school, work, hobbies—can be gathered together here. In a way, your wedding gives you and your fiancé a mirror into which you look and see all the people who really matter to you both. This in itself is an intoxicating thought: having so many people who care about you gathered together for the sole purpose of celebrating you and the man you've chosen to marry.

While the initial feelings of elation can function like an emotional drug, you have to be aware that your sense of intoxication may have a negative component as well.

Often, the elation people experience when they first become engaged is based on the unconscious notion that, finally, they have found the "good parent"— that is to say, the one who will love you in just the way you want and need to be loved. Yet this expectation lays the groundwork for future feelings of betrayal and disappointment: once again, the "good" parent has failed.

But you have to realize that the problem is less the failure of your partner than the expectation itself, which is unrealistic. Rarely can a husband or wife become the wished-for parent. By continuing to believe that he or she can, you are setting yourself up for disappointment from the outset.

◆

□ *Getting to Know You*

Whether you and your beloved have announced a formal engagement—pictures in the paper, engagement parties—you are nevertheless now engaged. But what does it mean *emotionally* to be engaged, especially as we move into the 1990s? In the long-distant past, the engagement allowed a couple to get to know each other; considering the number of arranged marriages, this was no doubt a crucial period.

But today, not only do you and your partner probably know each other intimately, it is very likely that you have lived together, or nearly so—many couples who maintain separate residences prior to getting married still find themselves spending most of their time together, at the home of one partner or the other—and you have probably had the opportunity to meet each other's friends and families. So many of the traditional motivations for the engagement period are no longer valid in quite the same way.

Yet there are still some important emotional—as well as practical—functions that the engagement period serves.

For one thing, it allows you and your prospective groom a chance to function together as a different kind of couple, with a greater sense of commitment. While you have certainly functioned as a couple before the engagement, once you have decided to get married, there are new imperatives to work out some of the old trouble spots between you.

For example, Molly, a twenty-seven-year-old account executive, describes her reactions to the two best friends of her fiancé, Jeff, this way: "I never liked Ted and Mark and so whenever I could, I avoided seeing them. I did encourage Jeff to see them alone, but when he tried to arrange a group event—their girlfriends were invited along—I still bowed out. But once we got engaged, I began to realize that avoiding them wasn't the answer. These two guys were important to Jeff, and I realized that if I loved him, I was going to have to learn to deal with them. And frankly, the early part of the engagement was the right time to begin thinking about all these issues.

"Before we were engaged I would have been too frightened of losing Jeff to have raised an issue as potentially upsetting as my feelings about his friends."

What is true for friends—his and yours—is also true for your families. Now is the time to start thinking about the relationships you have with each other's relatives. You should also give some thought to how you want to address your new in-laws after the wedding. While "Mom" and "Dad" have been considered standard forms of address for in-laws, this may seem too intimate for you, especially if your own parents are alive. First names are both appropriately close yet acknowledge the distance that does exist; many couples find this the best route. Another alternative is incorporating your in-laws' last name, e.g., "Mother Silver." But whatever you choose, this is a good time to start thinking and talking about how to address them, both with your fiancé and eventually, with the two families. (For more on the emotional significance of names, see chapter 6.)

□ *His and Hers*

Up to this point, most of the feelings that have been discussed could apply equally well to both partners. But it is also true that an engagement will evoke different responses in men and women, and those differences are well worth examining.

Despite the radical changes that have occurred in societal attitudes and expectations concerning the roles of the sexes, many women nevertheless still experience getting married as a sign of having been chosen, selected, and of being very, very special. This may come as a surprise, for like many contemporary women, your conscious ideas about yourself and your goals may well conflict with unconscious expectations, handed down from generations of myth, folklore, and fairy tale. Certainly, this was true for Carolyn, a thirty-seven-year-old physician with a hectic schedule at a major urban hospital: "For so long I had thought of myself in terms of my profession—being a doctor doesn't leave you room to think about much of anything else. And to make it through medical school, I had to downplay any of the ways in which I felt different from the men in my classes because the competition was so stiff. It's not that I didn't perceive myself as a woman—but I certainly didn't perceive myself as a woman with very conventional responses and reactions. So in a way I was unprepared for my feelings—a sense of being cherished, pampered, thoroughly adored and special—when I got engaged. It was a wild experience. Here I was, a hardworking, no-nonsense doctor, with a patient case load longer than my arm, and I was feeling like some goofy heroine of a 1950s musical comedy!"

Carolyn is pointing out what seems to be a very common phenomenon: the expectations women have about their careers are not always in line with the ones they have about personal relationships. And though you, like Carolyn, may not have thought much at all about getting married, or even seen it as a particular goal, once you have decided to do it, you may well find yourself experiencing some very traditional reactions. But then, as has been discussed earlier from a slightly different vantage point, getting married is a very traditional experience, and it will undoubtedly evoke many equally traditional responses.

It is especially important to understand these feelings, precisely because they may not at all be in keeping with what your fiancé is going through. While *you* may be feeling like a cross between Cinderella and Snow White, he may be feeling like something other than Prince Charming.

Although it is true that a man may experience an

elation similar to yours at this moment—he feels special, loved, uniquely cherished—he is also experiencing other feelings that may conflict with the purely positive ones. Again, putting aside the ways in which men have changed in recent years—being more capable of talking about feelings and expressing emotion—it is often the case that a man feels the atavistic thrill of conquest when he asks a woman to marry him and she says yes.

"I was pretty surprised at myself," says Jack, a thirty-four-year-old film maker. "I never thought of myself in those sexist, macho terms. I knew I loved Karen as a whole person, not as an object; I respected her wit, her intelligence, her integrity as much as I had ever respected anyone's. But when we decided to get married, I was shocked to find myself—at least inside—strutting around like some latter-day Tarzan. When we were out together, I wanted to tell strangers—okay, *male* strangers—'Hey, see this beautiful, sexy, brainy woman? Well, she's mine, so eat your heart out, fella!'"

But even in the midst of these powerfully charged positive feelings, your fiancé may be battling with a set of responses that will most likely be foreign to you.

Once again, societal changes notwithstanding, the concept of manhood still carries with it the emotional freight of isolation and singularity: for generations, being a man meant not being emotionally dependent, and many men unconsciously experience a residue of those messages. So at the very moment your partner is feeling thrilled, proud, and happy, he may also be feeling a threat to his manhood and his very sense of self.

There may be an even deeper explanation for his feelings of suffocation and violation. To get at the root of it, some theoretical discussion of psychological motivation may help. In infancy, both boys and girls are identified most closely with the person who gave them life: mother. But somewhere along the way, the little boy has to give up identification with mom in exchange for a more lasting identification with his father. In this context, marriage represents a symbolic reunion with a long-lost feminine principle. Of course, to a certain extent, marriage is a reunion for every woman with her father. But because boys have had to give up their mothers, the unconscious resonance of marriage is a reunion that is at once immensely satisfying but also fraught with fear at losing the very gender identification he worked so hard to win as an infant. If you find that your prospective groom seems especially touchy and insistent on his male prerogatives right now, fear not—it is probably just a healthy reassertion of his male identification.

Of course, this is only one of many anxieties—which will be discussed at much greater length in chapter 2—that both you and your fiancé will start to feel, but because this one is apt to start occurring even while the engagement elation still has you both flying high, it's worth mentioning now.

There are distinct differences in the way that men and women experience and express their emotions in general, which will of course affect how each of you will function during the engagement. The closer two people become, the more keenly they will experience the gender differences, as well as other differences. It's unavoidable.

In my experience, I have observed that men generally have more difficulty in talking about their feelings than women. Often, the only feeling that many men are comfortable expressing is anger, so that "feelings" and "anger" have become synonymous in their vocabularies. Expressing the more tender emotions has a negative connotation for these men—they fear they will be considered weak and sappy—that it doesn't have for women.

I think, as a woman, you need to understand the implications of this difference in order to suspend any negative judgments you may form about your fiancé. It's not that he won't talk about his feelings, but rather that he doesn't know how to yet.

◆

□ *Emotional Prep Time*

After you've made the commitment to get married, you are bound to feel a dozen unsettling and often conflicting emotions—some of them have already been discussed in this chapter, and just a quick look at the table of contents of this book will highlight several more—and it is therefore extremely important that you have a little time to prepare yourselves for the emotional changes that marriage demands without interference from other people. You're going to feel a lot of different emotions, and maintaining an initial degree of privacy about your decision will help you get ready to face them. Taking the necessary emotional space and time to prepare for the roller coaster ahead is one of the best presents you can give yourselves right now.

Once you've decided to get married, your first impulse may be to get on the phone and start calling everyone you know—even if it's 2 A.M. While the exuberance expressed by such a gesture is terrific, it may not actually be the best thing for you or for your relationship.

On the most practical level, it is all too easy to get swept up in the reactions and expectations of other people. Jean and Rob know that syndrome only too well: "As soon as we told my parents we were getting married, they immediately began planning the wedding for us—asking how many people we were having, where we would hold it, what color the bridesmaids dresses would be—there was no chance to relax and just enjoy the good feelings," Jean recalls. "I know my folks meant well, but we both agreed that if we could do it over, it would have been better to wait before telling everyone."

Even if your families aren't the types that tend to take over, you can easily get sucked into the planning process *yourselves*—the "business" of getting married—once you have made it real with announcements to the outside world. Strange as it may seem, you may have trouble with simply savoring this period; instead you may rush ahead to start scheduling, arranging, and organizing. Once again, if you don't rush to tell anyone that you're getting married, there will be less of a temptation to move from pleasurable feeling to concrete action. Take the time to delight in this new and special knowledge, without feeling pressured to do anything about it right away.

What to Do

Here are a few tips about how the two of you can use this special time in a very private, and yet highly constructive, way:

◆ Plan how you want to break the news to your respective families and friends; alone or together? In person or over the phone? There are pros and cons attached to each. Telling people your news while you are together emphasizes your union; this is a good alternative with family because you are making a statement about the new family unit you are now creating. But telling friends— especially ones your fiancé doesn't know well—might be better off done alone, to lessen the sense of exclusion that they might feel. (For more on dealing with friends, see chapter 4.)

Delivering your news in person is obviously the more intimate choice, yet if you sense you may get a negative reaction from any family members—more on this in chapter 3—the telephone gives you the chance to get on and off quickly. And it allows your parents (or any other family member) to deal with the news in their own way.

◆ Choose several alternative wedding dates and think about the positive and negative aspects of each. You may feel summer, with its promise of warmth and natural abundance, is the right time; yet since this is the season in which many people are away, you may face the possibility that certain members of the family and friends won't be able to attend. It is up to you to decide on how important such issues are and this is a good time to start thinking about them. However, you should *not* get any further involved in the planning at this stage.

◆ Have a special celebration all by yourselves—it can be a wonderful meal you make together or eat out, tickets to the theater, ballet, or concert, or a weekend getaway— in which you fully experience the new commitment you have just made to each other. For one couple it might mean two days in a tiny rural inn; for another, an extravagant night on the town. But the result will be the same: you will be able to celebrate the magic of getting married alone in your own special way.

◆ Share your fantasies about the "ideal" wedding you each envision. Again, don't focus on the actual planning yet, but instead use this time to explore what may be deeply buried hopes, wishes, and expectations.

Write these fantasies down and return to them later when you do make your actual plans. They may well help you to get back on course at a later stage when the many details and complications of planning a wedding have all but extinguished your initial elation.

2.

ANXIETY:

Having Second Thoughts

◆

☐ *Coming Down to Earth*

You've undoubtedly heard the phrase "What goes up must come down." Well, it is as true for the emotive life as it is for physics. You may well find that after the initial excitement, both you and your partner are beset by a whopping case of the post-elation blues.

Once the euphoria wears off and the reality sets in ("Am I really going to be married to this person for the rest of my life?"), second thoughts about the seriousness of your decision are common. And those second thoughts are likely to be followed by third, fourth, and fifth thoughts—when taken together, they add up to a massive case of anxiety.

"About three weeks after we had decided to get married, I just felt this overwhelming sense of panic," says twenty-eight-year-old Cora, an executive secretary with a multinational firm. "I looked at John—whom I'd known and loved for three years—and thought, 'Who is this person anyway? What in the world am I doing?' "

Cora's anxieties are hardly unique. Here are just a few of the more commonly heard post-elation second thoughts (don't be surprised if you hear yourselves saying them to each other, too!):

◆ "Why rock the boat? Things have been going so well between us."

◆ "We've seen so many unhappy marriages; who needs that?"

◆ "Isn't marriage death to romance?"

◆ "Why bother—we don't need to be married to have a sexual relationship or live together; our friends and families accept our situation comfortably."

◆ "It's so expensive to get married—we could use the money for something else."

◆ "The divorce rate is so high—why do we think we'll beat the odds?"

◆ "Sure you have to get married to have children, but we aren't planning to have them for quite some time."

◆ "One of us has been married before—why risk it again?"

□ *Don't Fight It*

But before you even begin to think about addressing your anxieties, it should be said that a certain (and note the key word here is *certain*) amount of anxiety during this period is not only natural, but even desirable, during the prewedding period. Getting married is a major life event and you are bound to feel some apprehension in anticipation of it. That doesn't mean your choice of mate is wrong or that you shouldn't be getting married; on the contrary, a modicum of anxiety attests to the fact that you understand the seriousness of what you're doing. "The only people who aren't nervous about getting married simply haven't thought about it at all!" says Ann, who has been happily wed for a year. "Before the wedding I had a lot of doubts, and Mike and I did our best to work through them. But having doubts didn't mean we weren't doing the right thing; in our case, it was our way of proving that we were."

□ *A Change in Tempo*

While some anxiety is perfectly natural, you nevertheless don't want your doubts and worries to overshadow the entire planning process, so you'll need to devise a few strategies for how to cope. One great way to deal with the onset of these anxieties is so obvious that you might easily overlook it: SLOW DOWN. If you stop to think about it, you'll realize that when you're anxious, the mental pace at which you are moving tends to be very rapid. Your mind is going a mile a minute; you're thinking of a dozen different things at the same time, all of which can seem threatening, problematic, even insurmountable.

Somewhere during this anxiety-prone period, you and your fiancé should set aside some time to express your doubts, no matter how insignificant they seem. Lock the door, take the phone off the hook, pull down the shades and prepare to spend some real time facing your anxieties. Each of you should make a list of everything that is worrying you, and then you should exchange lists. If you know that your fiancée is anxious about the cost of the wedding, you can keep his budgetary considerations in mind throughout the planning process. If he knows you're worried about dealing with your folks, he can help when it comes time to do that.

Clearing the air at every possible opportunity is always a good idea because unarticulated anxieties are potentially dangerous to the health of your relationship. As long as they remain in the fertile ground of your imagination, they can grow to alarming dimensions. Once exposed to the fresh air of mutual discussion, however, they will begin to assume their proper perspective. In so many instances, the clear articulation of your specific anxieties goes a long way toward dispelling them.

□ *The Unspoken Truths*

After you express all your anxieties to each other, there may still be nagging thoughts about your future spouse, or marriage in general, that you tend to keep to yourself. These are things you feel certain you can never say to your partner, and so they are even more upsetting because of the self-imposed sense of secrecy.

◆ "What about all the other men [women] I won't get to meet?"

◆ "He [she] is such a slob—am I going to have to endure those dirty socks [panty hose] strewn all over forever?"

◆ "I can't stand his [her] family!"

When it comes to private thoughts like these, their negative content alone is unsettling. But more than that, the very fact that you are having thoughts you feel can't be shared makes you feel guilty and lonely—two highly unexpected emotions at a time like this. *Anything* that makes you feel separate from your partner right now is particularly apt to raise the anxiety level several notches. This is a moment when you want to feel united, not divided.

It helps to recognize that it is precisely the enormity of the impending union that is creating the anxiety in the first place, and causing you to draw away. And part of getting back on track is the sharing of these seemingly unmentionable subjects with your partner.

Of course, this has to be done with a great deal of diplomacy and tact, as the tension may be running high between the two of you. And you will also have to be prepared to listen to your partner's worst anxieties; the permission to vent has to go in both directions to really be effective. But you will find that verbalizing the "un-mentionables" can actually bring you closer if you handle it right. Here are some ways to navigate the chancy seas of mutual confession:

◆ *Take responsibility for your own feelings.* Start off your sentences with the word "I." Phrases like "I feel you don't hear me when . . ."; "I need for you to . . ."; "I want you to . . ."; "I like/don't like when you . . ." are all good ways to begin any discussion. The reason? Such language puts the emphasis squarely on *your* feelings and desires—subjects you are entirely justified in discussing. But if you begin with the word "you," as in: "You are impossible . . ."; "You always/you never . . ."; "Why don't you ever listen to me . . . ?"; and "You should . . . ," it will sound judgmental and your partner is apt to be more defensive and less responsive.

◆ *Choose your time wisely.* Don't start a serious discussion at meal times, when people are due over, when your partner is exhausted or under a great deal of stress in another area of his life (job, family, etc.). Instead, wait for a time when you can be alone, undisturbed, and have ample energy to be attentive to one another and time to finish what you have started.

◆ *Be conscious of your body language and facial expressions.* Crossed arms, a defiant stance, frowning, and pouting will all conspire to make your partner feel attacked and unable to listen. If possible, smile once in a while or at least try to keep your expression neutral. And a squeeze on the arm or a gentle pat probably will help in getting your point across.

◆ *Don't "globalize."* Make an effort to stick to one emotional issue at a time, so your partner can absorb and respond to what you're saying. If you try to deal with everything that is on your mind all at once, he is going to feel a sense of emotional overload.

☐ *Second Time Around*

If either your or your fiancé has been married before, the upcoming wedding will create a very particular type of anxiety. "Chris was so plagued with bitterness about the end of his first marriage," says twenty-nine-year-old Janet. "As we planned the wedding I began to feel that he was blaming me for all of her mistakes." But happily enough, Chris and Janet were able to get through the difficult period, a process that was in large part facilitated by Janet. "I made him tell me all the ways in which he felt she had failed him. Then I compared—point by point—our relationship. Once Chris realized that he and I had a different kind of relationship, he was able to look toward the future with a renewed optimism."

Bitterness against *all* women—or all men—is one kind of anxiety that surfaces during the prewedding period; fear of failing in a second marriage is yet another. "I knew that I loved Tim and wanted to marry him," says thirty-five-year-old Paula, "but I kept thinking—what if it doesn't work out? I just can't go through another divorce—it was so painful the first time. I don't want to be a two-time loser."

Yet, statistically speaking, couples marrying for a second time have the odds in their favor: According to recent data, they are far less likely to undergo divorce. "I'll say 'Amen' to that," says forty-three-year-old Cathy, whose second marriage is now two years old. "Craig and I both had been through such hell in our first marriages—his first wife played around; my ex-husband was a compulsive gambler—we were determined to do it right this time. At least all that misery taught us something. Had we let the fear of the past inhibit us from getting married, we never would have known the happiness that we feel now."

If you are a second-time bride, try the following this time:

◆ Consciously strive to make this wedding different from the last one: If your first wedding was a three-hundred-guest extravaganza, consider a smaller, more-intimate second wedding. If your parents assumed almost complete control of the planning the first time around, then make a concerted effort to assert your wishes for round two.

◆ Discourage family (big culprits here!) and friends from making comparisons between your first husband and your fiancé. Keep the past in its place, and encourage them to do the same.

◆ Talk openly to your fiancé about your anxieties: The more you are able to talk about any residual bitterness, fear, anger, the less likely you are to act out these things in your behavior toward him. If he's the one who has been married before, encourage the same kind of frankness.

□ *Tip of the Iceberg*

You also need to realize that all the second thoughts you are having are probably symptomatic of the larger areas of difference that form the background to even the happiest of couplings. The major differences that exist now will continue to exist in one form or another throughout your life together but now—on the eve of marriage—you may be feeling more anxious about them than ever before. Here are some of the more significant areas of difference that you and your partner may be facing:

• *Religion.* Even though a difference in religions may not have caused problems until this point, the divergence will inevitably arise when you decide to get married, both because of the nature of the ceremony and the upbringing of your children—should you be planning to have them—are contingent upon how you handle it. Chapter 7 will deal with this issue in much greater detail.

• *Race.* According to the U.S. Bureau of the Census, interracial marriages are on the rise in the United States. Obviously, if you and your partner are from different races, you've thought long and hard about your decision to join your lives together, and have undoubtedly come up against some major disapproval (see chapter 3 for more on this subject). Interracial couples have unusual pressures brought to bear on them, and so you should understand that your anxiety level is apt to be at an all-time high right now. What is also important to recognize is that you may be expressing that anxiety in other, less-direct ways: You may find yourself newly critical of your partner's friends, his attitude toward domestic chores, etc., as a way of expressing your deeper anxieties about the choice you are making.

• *Socio-economics.* This can be problematic, because there is not necessarily a way to "handle" a difference in socio-economic background. Lots of tension may arise from the outside, that is to say, family and friends. Though no one likes to use the word "class" in this country, there is nevertheless a persistent and real difference in people's backgrounds, manners, and ways of doing things. Nancy, a twenty-five-year-old history graduate student, is from a highly cultivated, though far from wealthy, family. Her fiancé, Leo, comes from a much more affluent background, but lacks the kind of social grace and finesse that Nancy had been taught to admire. "Leo is truly the salt of the earth," she says. "I know him to be a very decent, caring human being. But sometimes those *nouveau riche* affectations of his—the showy car, the leather coat—are obnoxious. I love him, but I wonder if I can put up with all his pretensions."

• *Education.* Like differences in background, a disparity between your educational background and that of your partner may well be a cause for anxiety during the prewedding period. "I know Ben doesn't think less of me as a person because I attended a state university," says

Tracey, a twenty-nine-year-old owner of a small travel agency, "but sometimes I think that his fancy, Ivy League education will catch up with him and he'll wish he married someone from Vassar or one of those places."

◆ *Age.* Couples in which there is a significant difference in ages (more than ten years) may well get cold feet before the wedding. As a woman of thirty marrying a man of forty-five, you might well think "He'll be an old man while I'm still a young woman; will I have to take care of him?" or "I'll be left alone someday." As a woman of forty marrying a man of thirty, you might wonder, "Will he get tired of me and want to find someone younger?" or "What if he decides he wants children later on and it's too late for me to have them?" These are very real considerations, and although you have probably thought about them before, they are probably particularly unsettling right now. But it's important to keep in mind that you are never given a guarantee about the future of a relationship, no matter what the ages of the people involved. Some marriages between couples of differing ages are blissfully happy; others are not. But so far, no one has proved that the statistics are any better for couples who are closer together in age.

◆ *Sexual needs.* Chances are, if you and your partner have radically different ideas about what constitutes a good sex life, you wouldn't be planning to get married at all. But what about those times *lately* when he's either too aloof or too insistent? Now that you're ready to wed, these little differences may seem particularly troublesome. "He used to be so passionate," complains thirty-year-old Maggie, "but as soon as we decided to tie the knot, he practically became bashful in bed!"

Maggie—and you—need to understand that the prewedding anxiety is apt to put a damper on even the most ardent of couples; in general, feeling nervous isn't much of an aphrodisiac. It is unlikely—indeed, well nigh impossible—that you and your partner will be on the same sexual wavelength all the time, anyway. Don't exaggerate any little differences now; remember that the tension can easily inhibit your libido or his. Instead, if you're both feeling jumpy, move the emphasis away from sex and onto other, less emotionally charged forms of intimacy and communication.

It is not unusual for engaged couples to experience a diminished interest in sex during the prewedding period; consequently, you and your fiancé may temporarily lose your desire for one another. Because there is so much anxiety about sexuality in general, this may be one more thing you feel worried about, and it is easy to interpret—wrongly—your decreased desire as a purely sexual problem.

It's important to understand that the real anxiety stems from the nature of the commitment you have just made to one another. You may be frightened by it, and for that reason, feel the need to move away from each other. The result: a decreased sexual appetite.

You may also be experiencing anxiety over the im-

pending "loss of self" that marriage entails. By this I mean the fear that you will lose your autonomy and emotional independence by getting married. It's quite common for both men and women to feel the threat of being swallowed or enveloped by the other person, and the natural reaction to that feeling may be to pull away for a time. This can also translate into a decreased sexual drive. Since sex is about merger and togetherness and in a sense requires some loss of self, this may be precisely the reason that you (or your partner) are not interested in it right now.

Also, given the physiologically determined sexual roles that men and women must contend with, the transition into sexuality may become more difficult and conflict-laden, which in turn can result in a decrease in desire. By this I mean that despite all the societal changes of the last twenty years, the sexual act has not changed. Men are still required to get and maintain an erection; women must be open and receptive if sexual intercourse is to happen.

Yet this male-assertive/female-receptive physiological dynamic is often in conflict with the other, more homogenized emotional roles that men and women assume in their daily lives. The male/female roles are no longer so clear: Men are now often the primary caretakers for the children when their wives are the primary breadwinners. But as far as the sexual act goes, the physiology hasn't changed: the man must be the active, assertive partner and the woman, the open, receptive one. As a result, there may be a good deal of confusion and difficulty that arises

29

around the issue of sexuality. A natural response to this confusion is a falling off in sexual appetite.

◆

Maggie became so frustrated with Ethan's postengagement lack of ardor that she finally started to express her dissatisfaction. But she went about it in all the wrong ways. To start, her timing was bad: She first broached the subject the evening that Ethan learned he had been passed over for a promotion. If there was anything he didn't need at this moment, it was the pressure to prove he was a "real man." Not surprisingly, the effect was exactly the opposite of what Maggie had hoped for. Not only did Ethan feel decidedly unsexual, he accused Maggie of being in conspiracy with his boss to undermine his self-confidence. Timing wasn't her only problem—her delivery was less than sensitive. Instead of waiting for a moment when she could discuss the matter calmly and without interruption, she lodged her complaints when both of them were exhausted, and she became impatient and shrill. Ethan couldn't possibly focus on the content of what she was saying. All he heard was an angry and tired fiancée berating him yet again.

Let Maggie be a lesson to you. There are more- and less-effective methods of getting your message across. Here are a few guidelines that can serve as examples. In each case, the goal is to avoid making a judgment about your partner; put emphasis where it belongs—on how *you* feel.

What *Not* to Say	What to Say Instead
You're not satisfying me.	I miss the sexual intimacy we used to have.
There must be something wrong with you.	I'm wondering if something is bothering you.
I guess you don't find me very sexy anymore.	Is there something that I could do that you'd find especially sexy right now?

☐ *"You like tomato and I like tomahto..."*

In addition, you are probably aware of the more subtle, but nevertheless important, areas of emotional difference that have always presented problems and will not cease to do so simply because you are now engaged to be married.

"Todd has a tremendous need to have other people around him all the time," says Margo of her fiancé. "I'm a much more private person, and sometimes the constant socializing puts too much pressure on me. Not only that, I feel the need to be all by myself, away from him, sometimes, which he always interprets as rejection, even though it's not. I'm anxious that when we get married, these problems are going to get worse and not better."

"Pete and I can never agree on a movie or even a TV show that we both want to see. We have two televisions and two VCRs, and we haven't seen a film together in the last four years. It's almost gotten to be a kind of joke between us," says Marie, who is thirty-one, in describing her relationship of five years, "but now that we're getting married, I'm wondering: Do little things like this indicate some more serious way in which Peter and I are unsuited?"

"Jim is such an archconservative!" complains Suzanne about her fiancé. "One-to-one, he's such a terrific person, but sometimes his political opinions get me furious."

These kinds of issues—differences in needs for privacy and the company of other people, taste in books, movies, politics—are less divisive than the larger ones of religion, race, and the like. And yet they may be causing you tremendous anxiety right now, for reasons that Marie has articulated: You wonder whether the small areas of disagreement are indications of larger ones down the road.

In fact, this is a question that can't really be answered at this juncture, although it is worth posing. For some couples, the small differences are a signal of something more serious to come. But for most people, dwelling on the little things is just a way of deflecting attention from the general anxiety about getting married. It can't be overemphasized that getting married represents a major life change, and any important change, even when positive and welcome, elicits anxiety. Just be aware of this tendency toward emotional displacement. You and your partner may well find yourselves being super critical of each other, and especially worried about any minor disagreements and differences precisely because you *are* about to be joined in such a profound way.

□ *Dispelling the Fantasies*

It is also important to understand that many of the more romantic fantasies you may have about love—built up over years from the accumulated impact of fairy tales, myths, novels, plays, films, and poetry—can actually get in the way of your relationship as you live in it on a daily basis.

The paradigm of love that is set forth in these artistic works is one of perfect complicity, union, and mergence. Tristan couldn't live without Isolde; Romeo chose to die without Juliet, Anthony's life without Cleopatra was unendurable—the stories change, but the message is the same: To be in love is to be inseparable, and indeed, to feel as if the two of you are one person. Life in the absence of the beloved becomes meaningless and not worth living.

While all this may sound terribly romantic in theory, it becomes a highly confusing model when you try to apply it to everyday life. The fact is, as much as you love your partner, the two of you are *not* the same person. Therefore, it is unrealistic to believe that you will always feel alike or see eye-to-eye on all issues. But because this fantasy is so pervasive, you may feel anxious over any differences, be they major or minor, that divide you from your fiancé.

□ *Separate But Equal*

One of the very first, and perhaps even the best, ways to deal with your differences is simply to acknowledge them. There is nothing to be gained by substituting wishful thinking for the separate but equal realities of your different psyches. Despite the Hollywood myths to the contrary, there is no couple on earth who is undivided on every issue and attitude. Sometimes, as the old saying goes, you have to agree to disagree. And sometimes you have to disagree to agree: A good relationship is made of the dynamic that is created by the coming together of two strong and fully formed personalities. While you're trying to grapple with your very real and necessary points of difference, try to keep in mind the following:

◆ Focus on the things that you do share, such as a mutual love for great food, forties films, exotic travel, sports, pets, even something as humdrum as crossword puzzles or a particular TV show.

◆ Understand that you love your partner *for,* not just *despite* your differences. In fact, these differences are what may actually permit you to be a couple. The tranquillity of his temperament may be a welcome relief from the nonstop intensity of your own; your methodical nature is a perfect counterpoint to his somewhat more scattered approach.

Though you may occasionally find that a quality of his annoys you, if you think about all its permutations, you'll realize that that same quality is also what can bring you solace and joy. For instance, a man who is socially passive and unwilling to express his opinions strongly in company, may, in that context, appear dull. But that same man may also be the one who gives you complete freedom to express *your* thoughts and opinions, as vigorously and as forcefully as you want. When looked at in this way, that same quality could seem liberating and wonderful.

◆ Take heart from the fact that if you didn't really love one another a lot, you wouldn't even be at this stage in your relationship.

Although it is a discouraging fact, it must be stated that not every couple who gets engaged actually ends up getting married. The anxieties which surface during the prewedding period are troubling enough to make some couples change their minds about each other. That's what happened for Henry and Jane, a couple in their late twenties who decided to get married after a four-year romance.

"I found out a lot of things about him that I didn't admire or even like," said Jane ruefully. "For instance, the way he let his parents completely take over—it made me feel that he wasn't an adult. And I didn't like the way he was treating me. He was so annoyed by all aspects of the wedding preparations and acted as if I had contrived the decisions—which we had to make after all—simply to annoy him. Getting married had been his idea, but he wasn't willing to take responsibility for it. Instead, he either blamed me for being a nag, or he wanted his mother to take care of everything. Breaking up was sad, but since I'm convinced we would have come to this point anyway, I'm glad we did it sooner, rather than after the wedding."

But for other couples, deciding not to get married may not spell the end of the romance. Susanna, a free-lance beauty consultant, had been living with her banker boyfriend Perry for two years when the subject of marriage first came up. She was thirty-seven and he was thirty-three; both felt that they knew what they wanted and what they wanted was each other. But soon after they told their respective families that they had decided to get married, Perry withdrew so completely that Susanna was left wondering what had happened to the man she loved. "He was moody and unresponsive," she recalls. "We went from having a really thrilling, active sex life to having no sex at all. And the worst part was not being able to get through to him: He just wouldn't talk about his feelings at all."

Finally, though, Perry broke down and told Susanna he just couldn't go through with the wedding. The idea of getting married made him feel trapped beyond his worst fears. He said he didn't blame Susanna if she left him; he knew he had hurt her but he was unable to act any differently.

Susanna's first impulse was to leave: "He had his chance," she said, but something told her to hang on. She and Perry had had such a good thing before the issue of marriage was mentioned, she didn't want to be hasty in ending the relationship. So Susanna stayed with Perry and, gradually, the harmony in their relationship returned. Not long ago, they moved to Minneapolis, where Perry was offered a great job. They're talking about marriage again, though neither one feels ready quite yet to move from talk to action.

What's the moral of this story? Just this: Even if the prewedding anxieties prove to be too much for you, it doesn't mean you aren't made for each other, or that you won't, in time, get married. Some couples just need a few trial runs before they make it through to the finish line.

☐ *Worst-Case Scenario*

When trying to get at your anxieties, it sometimes helps to verbalize the worst situation you can imagine as a way of defusing its power. "I kept asking myself, 'What's the worst thing that could happen if we got married?" said Cora, who was quoted earlier at the beginning of this chapter, "and my answer finally was, 'We could get divorced.'" But as John pointed out to me, one of us could also be stricken with a terrible illness or get hit by a bus—in that context, divorce hardly seemed so terrible. I guess it was important to say the thing that was on both our minds: 'What if it doesn't work out?' But once you've said that, and realize that although divorce would be terrible it wouldn't by any means be the worst thing that could happen, you're able to relax a little. Sure getting married is a risk—but after all, what isn't?"

3.

RESISTANCE:

Telling the Families

◆

While the emotions of elation and anxiety center primarily around you and your fiancé, the emotions of resistance and jealousy—discussed in this chapter and the next—are ones that emerge when you extend your focus to the larger circle of family and friends.

□ *Where It All Began*

There is every reason to assume that telling your parents you are getting married will win their unqualified approval. After all, in entering the married state you are validating the decision they made so long ago and of which you are the result. To return to the source and announce your impending marriage would seem as complete a ratification of your own family history as can be imagined. And for some couples, this is exactly what happens: Mom and Dad react to the big news with all the enthusiasm and delight you would have wished.

But other, less fortunate (though just as typical) couples may be in for a rude awakening. The very same parents who seem to have wanted nothing more than your marriage may now exhibit some rather surprising forms of resistance when you tell them you *are* getting married.

□ *Guess Who's Coming to Dinner?*

The parental resistance you encounter is usually of two basic kinds. The most obvious, and by far the most painful and destructive, is outright disapproval of your chosen partner. Needless to say, this is an extremely difficult situation in which to find yourself. The feeling is one of being torn in two: You obviously love your fiancé and are not about to give him up, but you also love your family and want their approval of your choice.

Your parents may resist accepting your chosen life partner because of his age, race, religion, choice of profession, background, or education. But no matter what their objections, the bottom line is that you are not about to give up your fiancé to accommodate your family. For that reason, you need to find ways to get your parents to accept your choice simply because it is your choice, even if they disapprove of the individual person you have chosen.

Mona and Dean have an interesting story to tell about serious parental resistance. Dean, who is fifteen years older than Mona, had originally been a friend of her father's. Both men were astronomers who taught at the same West Coast university and moved in the same, rather tightly knit professional circle. While Mona's parents had always enjoyed Dean's company socially, they were in no way pleased to find out that he had become romantically involved with their daughter. And when Mona and Dean announced their engagement, her parents hit the ceiling. "My mother actually called him up to tell him she thought he was taking advantage of me," recalled Mona, who is now twenty-seven. "She wanted him to break things off immediately." When it became clear that Mona and Dean were not about to dissolve their relationship, her parents showed their displeasure by refusing to participate in planning the wedding. "Never mind about helping to pay for it," said Mona, "my mother wouldn't even go with me to the florist." Finally, in a last-ditch effort to change their daughter's mind, Mona's parents threatened to boycott the wedding.

"When they did that, something inside me snapped," said Mona. "At first, I just tried to ignore their bad feelings about Dean. I figured that if they weren't going to help, I could just go ahead and start making the preparations by myself. But the idea that they actually wouldn't show up at my wedding was so upsetting to me that I knew I had to change my tactics."

This change in tactics involved meeting the parental resistance on all fronts. Dean and Mona spent hours with her parents, discussing the marriage and why her parents were so opposed to it. Dean also met with each of her parents individually. Mona's older sister, who thought Dean was a terrific guy, was also recruited. Together, she and Mona were able to stress the importance of preserving the family unit and make her parents see what they were doing by resisting. "Instead of just ignoring my mother, I swallowed my pride and told her how much her refusal to get involved in the wedding plans was hurting me. More than anything else I said to her, that really seemed to get through."

Slowly, Mona's parents began to accept the situation and even came to appreciate the sensitivity displayed by their future son-in-law. Pretty soon, Mona's mother was accompanying her on trips to the dressmaker's, and when the wedding day came, both of Mona's parents were there to share her joy.

Of course, not all stories of parental disapproval and resistance end so happily. Your parents may simply not work to overcome their prejudices, and they may ultimately refuse to accept the man you have chosen. Mona and Dean had the right idea in trying to obtain the participation of her parents, and you should use their story as a model. But if it doesn't work, don't start blaming yourself. Getting married is a way of separating yourself from your parents, and if they don't approve of your choice, you, like your parents, have to accept that separation, no matter how difficult it seems. Nor does this mean that their bad feelings will remain intact forever.

While Mona and Dean tried to address each of her parents' concerns individually, it may not always be wise to do so with your own parents. After all, you don't have to convince them, because they are not in a position to forbid your marriage. But it is a good idea to discuss their objections with your partner in a very specific fashion. If you can tell your fiancé "My mother thinks you're too young for me" or "My father is worried that you haven't settled into a profession or a career yet," you may well rid yourself of any lingering doubts that you have had and were not expressing. Letting your parent be the mouthpiece for your own anxieties may actually help your relationship during this period. You and your partner will feel more confident of your decision to get married if you have fully answered these objections to yourselves.

But sometimes you have to accept that you cannot and will not overcome your parents' objections; in that case, trying to address their concerns on an individual basis just won't help. If your parents are seriously bothered by a difference in religion—your fiancé is Christian and you are Jewish, for example—but *you* are much less concerned about this fact, you may never be able to successfully banish all their objections. Here, time is your best ally. Insofar as possible, encourage them to get involved in the wedding plans and be sure they are active participants in the day. Later, your continued happiness and well-being will be the best medicine in helping them overcome any residual resistance to your mate.

If his parents don't like you, you need to encourage him to deal with them in the ways that have been described here. Remember, you cannot—nor should you be expected to—resolve his relationship to his family. In fact, you will probably be resented all the more by his family if you attempt to intervene in his dealings with them.

□ *Hidden Agendas*

Sometimes, the resistance is not about whom you are marrying, but about the fact that you are marrying at all. Again, this may seem odd, given that your parents have been asking "When are you going to settle down and get married?" for as long as you can remember.

First of all, you must keep in mind that there is really no such thing as a "pure" emotion or a simple one either, for that matter; in fact, it is the nature of emotions to be complicated and often murky. Your parents may indeed be both delighted that you are getting married, and at the same time, more than a little resistant to the idea.

But is is equally important to understand that this kind of resistance is more likely to be about your parents—their particular worries, fears, difficulties, apprehensions—than about you or your fiancé at all. Here are some of the major issues that your upcoming wedding forces your parents to confront:

◆ *Growing old.* Since getting married undeniably makes you an adult, your parents are suddenly forced to accept the fact that you, their "child," is fully grown up. And your having grown up means that they have grown old. Even though they want your happiness, because it also makes them confront their own mortality—not an easy thought for anyone, under any circumstances—they may well display their resistance to the event.

◆ *Dynastic concerns.* Since children are the next logical step after marriage, your parents are undoubtedly evaluating your fiancé in terms of his suitability as the father of *their* grandchildren. Should you have children, you and your husband will be creating their inheritors and their connection to immortality. Naturally, they are bound to have a lot of strong feelings about the man you marry, but the fact is they have little control over whom you eventually choose. It is this lack of control about what they unconsciously perceive as their own future that is apt to make them difficult and obstinate about your chosen partner.

◆ *"We wanted you to marry a doctor!"* Parents often are guilty of projecting their own wishes and desires onto the lives of their children, and by extension, their children's mates. Since your parents may well be trying to live through you, they are subject to feeling disappointed when you reject the fantasy they have spun for your future.

◆ *Displacement from the center of your world.* Your upcoming marriage means that your parents are no longer the center of your emotional world; you are now going to have an equally powerful emotional connection to someone other than Mom and Dad. Unconsciously, your parents sense this gradual moving away and they can often resent it. Since they are feeling as if their control has been threatened, they may try to assert it all the more vigorously in this prewedding period. What for you is a union with another adored person, for them is a rupture within the family unit.

Not only does the marriage of a daughter or son change the family structure, in a more direct way—and this may surprise you—it often radically affects the marriage of your parents. For instance, if you have traditionally been called upon to play peacemaker between your squabbling parents, your own marriage may be unconsciously threatening to your parents because they sense you will be less available to them. Now that you are creating a family of your own, your ability to perform that function for them will be diminished. The conscious effect of all this is that your parents may raise objections to your marriage.

There are also other commonly held roles that children assume between their parents. Some of these can be described as: the Negotiator—the child who acts as a go-between or mediator in parental quarrels; the Scapegoat—the child who is unconsciously blamed for many of the parents' marital troubles; the Therapist—the child who is asked to listen to the problems of one or both parents; the Rationale—the child who is used by the parents as their reason for remaining together. In each of these cases, the marriage of the child is a direct threat to the way the parents' marriage has been structured. And as a consequence, parents may protest about the chosen partner, or any other aspect of the wedding, in an effort to retain the status quo.

◆

What to Do

Keep telling yourself that first and foremost the wedding is for you and your beloved. Consequently, while the needs, expectations, and desires of your parents (and his) are important, they should never be paramount. This is an important point and one that cannot be overemphasized: You are inviting your families to share your happiness, but they are not the center of it.

That having been said, it is nevertheless true that unhappy parents can seriously threaten—and even ruin—the joy of your wedding day. So while you want to be firm, you also have to know how to negotiate. Below, you will find three essential rules for coping with parental resistance without sacrificing your own desires.

RULE ONE: *Keep both sets of parents involved in— but don't let them dominate—all stages of the wedding planning.*

While maintaining the important prerogatives for yourselves, don't compromise on key issues like what kind of ceremony, general character of the event, or anything else that you feel is vital to your own sense of happiness about the day, but do invite your parents to participate in the decision-making process. As you move through this period keep in mind that the assertion and reassertion of the family unit is all-important, especially as it is about to be redefined by the addition of your soon-to-be husband and his family. Keeping your parents involved in the planning will go a long way toward helping them accept what is, after all, inevitable. If you keep them at a distance, you are only driving a greater wedge between them and the two of you. Sooner or later, there has to be a joining of the ways, and the best time to start is *now*.

Note: If your mother is calling you three times a day to talk about the guest list, you may already feel that she is involved enough in your wedding plans. But the taking of liberties is not the same thing as intimacy freely given. In this case, your mother's involvement is not at your express invitation; if she is to feel wanted, you have to make her feel that way by initiating the contact. When the hierarchy of giving and taking is kept clear in the wedding planning process, everyone will be happier for it.

RULE TWO: *Reward your parents for good behavior.*
This may sound silly in theory, but it is actually very important in practice. Whenever your mother or father (or one of *his* parents) does something that you find truly helpful and satisfactory to both your needs—your mother gets estimates from the caterers you have selected; your father offers to buy several cases of your favorite champagne for the wedding reception—thank them sincerely and without reservation. Your heartfelt thanks accomplishes two things: It makes your gratitude concrete, thus letting them know how much they have pleased you, and it also unconsciously encourages them to continue their behavior. After all, everyone—and parents are certainly included here—likes being rewarded with a compliment and seeks to repeat the experience.

RULE THREE: *Make sure that you and your future spouse function together; don't let the parental bickering create a rift between the two of you.*

That means, the two of you must sit down and decide *ahead of time* what is most important, so that you can maintain a united front against the disapproving parents. Otherwise, it is too easy to get caught between your parents and your future spouse, as Linda and Dick know all too well. Before consulting with Dick, Linda promised her mother that she would have a receiving line at the wedding. Only after she had given her word did she learn from Dick that the one thing he *didn't* want at the wedding was a receiving line; it was simply too formal and stiff for his taste. Linda then found herself in the awkward position of trying to mediate between her mother and her future husband. Her mother was upset because Linda had gone back on her word; Dick was hurt that she had made a promise without consulting him. The lesson here is clear: Don't make decisions, plans, or promises as an individual; keep in mind that now, more than ever, learning to function as a team is vital to your future happiness.

□ *Footing the Bill*

Traditionally, not only did the bride's parents pay for the entire wedding, they sweetened the pot by contributing the heftiest dowry they could afford. But times have indeed changed. There are, alas, no longer any rules about who pays for the wedding—which opens the door to emotional confusion and a very particular brand of parental resistance. Here, the resistance may work in an unexpected way: Your parents (or his) may insist on helping to pay for the wedding as a way of unconsciously trying to exert control over the event itself.

Despite changed attitudes and expectations, there are nevertheless many mothers and fathers of the bride who pay for the wedding as a matter of course. This is the way *their* parents did it, and they simply wouldn't have it any other way. While you may find such an alternative a relief from the very real pressure of financing your own wedding, as you probably understand by now, letting your (or his) parents pay for the wedding gives them more control over the shape the event will take. Put very simply: You may find it hard to argue with someone about the seating arrangements or the menu when that same person is picking up the tab.

Be that as it may, the traditional scenario in which the bride's parents pay for everything is well on its way to becoming a thing of the past, particularly as your parents may have already helped with a college and even graduate-level education. In the past, brides couldn't afford to pay for their own weddings; now, many of you can, and want to. Since today's bride and groom are likely to be older and more solidly established in their chosen careers, this makes the idea of paying for the wedding viable, whereas at one time it wasn't.

All this results in a situation where the financing of your wedding is now up for grabs. If you do pay for it yourselves, you are acccepting a greater burden (both financially and emotionally), but you are also gaining a greater freedom. There is no right or wrong choice here; just bear in mind that the degree of parental contribution is in direct proportion to the number of parental prerogatives assumed. If you want to make sure that the wedding plans remain squarely in your hands, your best bet is to finance it yourselves. But even if you accept parental help, do so with the understanding that you may need to reassert your control over the event's direction many times during the planning process.

☐ *Clash of the Titans*

Sometimes, resistance is less an issue between you and your family (or your fiancé and his), than between the two families themselves. The same major differences that cause your parents to question your choice—age, race, religion, socio-economic background, education, politics, values—may also cause problems between the two sets of in-laws. Or the problem may be more subtle than that: Your mother thinks his father is loud and overbearing; his parents think yours are showy and ostentatious. Whatever the source, you and your fiancé will need to find some way to deal with sparring families and the list below is a good place to begin:

♦ Plan event-oriented gatherings (barbecue, theatre party, card game, swimming party) to give the group something other than themselves on which to focus.

♦ Consider inviting other people along to prewedding

family events—your close friends and his are a good choice—as a way of diluting tensions. There is no reason that family gatherings must remain strictly so, especially if family members don't really get along.

◆ Give families separate but equal time: Decide to visit with your family Christmas eve; visit with his on Christmas day. Think of this as a "divide and conquer" strategy. There is no need to insist on everyone being together if the result is truly uncomfortable for all concerned.

◆ Keep in mind that your goal is simply to have people get along—you want the wedding day to run smooth as silk. You are not obligated to make people like each other, only to get them to behave cordially for a brief period of time.

□ *Oh Brother!*

Telling your brothers and sisters that you are getting married may not be as emotionally charged as telling your parents, but you nevertheless want them to express approval, support, and love when you deliver the news. And in many cases, that is just the reaction you'll get.

But sometimes, your brother or sister is apt to display his or her own brand of resistance to your getting married. There are a couple of main reasons for this, and they all have to do with jealousy. And while jealousy is a topic covered extensively in the next chapter, it is worth saying a few words about that special feeling between brothers and sisters, more commonly known as "sibling rivalry," in this context.

Since your wedding is going to elicit all kinds of feelings from your parents (some positive and others less so), the result is that all their attention is focused on you, not on your sibling(s). And because the central drama of most childhood sibling relationships is getting—and keeping—mommy and daddy's attention, your wedding may evoke all kinds of unpleasant past associations from your sister or brother. For that reason, a sibling may well appear disgruntled by the idea of your marriage. But this is not the only form of resistance to arise.

If you are marrying ahead of an older sister, she may feel jealous that your turn has come around first, before hers. And a younger sister who has watched you enviously from the wings for years may feel, yet again, "Here she goes, stealing the show!" Even a married sister may compare your future spouse to hers, giving rise to all sorts of feelings of competitiveness and jealousy. Nor are brothers immune to such feelings. Just because you are not of the same gender doesn't mean that there aren't powerful feelings of sibling rivalry.

What to Do

How you handle a sibling's resistance to your getting married depends a lot on what your relationship has been up to this point. If you are close and have enjoyed the kind of candor that makes talking about feelings of resistance and jealousy possible, then by all means do so. But you may not feel comfortable telling a sister or brother that you think he or she is jealous. In that case, it is important to try to include your sister or brother as a way of overcoming the jealousy and feelings of being left out. Here are some ways of accomplishing that:

◆ Give your sister or brother (this goes for your fiancé's siblings, too) a role in the ceremony: bridesmaid, best man, flower girl, ring bearer. Of course, if you have more than one sibling, this could open the door to still more-intense sibling rivalry, so you need to be mindful. "Since I have three sisters, I asked them all to be bridesmaids," says twenty-four-year-old Lucinda. "I was the first one in our family to be getting married and I didn't want any of them to feel left out. I decided to ask my best friend to be my maid of honor—that way, I was not forced to choose one sister over the others. Everyone seemed to think that was just fine."

◆ Ask your sister or brother for emotional and even practical support in dealing with your parents, much in the way that Mona did with hers. While it is true that siblings are divided by childhood rivalry, you may also find your sister or brother very sympathetic to your problems with your parents; after all, they have the same mother and father as you do, and have doubtless encountered some of the same difficulties. "My sister and I—sworn enemies since childhood—actually started getting close for the first time before my wedding," recounts Ronnie. "She had gotten married two years earlier, and my folks drove her crazy because her fiancé wasn't Catholic. When I got engaged to someone Jewish—at least *her* husband was Christian—my parents were wild. But she had been through it all before, and she was able to help. I guess she felt sorry for me and was able to open up about all kinds of things."

◆ Plan to spend some time alone with your sister or brother and your fiancé. If your sibling has a spouse or a "significant other," invite that person, too, but skip the parents. Let this be an occasion for members of the same generation to meet on equal ground. You may find that without parental expectations coming into play, you and your sibling are actually able to function as equals and even as friends.

☐ *Your Extended Families*

Resistance can come from all sectors of the family circle, not just the immediate one. Your parents may adore your future spouse and not care a whit that you and he don't share the same religion, but your elderly grandmother may be more difficult to convince.

Coping with the resistance of other family members—grandparents, aunts, uncles, godparents, and the like—requires the same patience and diplomacy that you used in dealing with your immediate family; sometimes, if they are very old and set in their ways, even more.

At all possible points, try to include the resistant family member in the wedding plans as a way of overcoming his or her negative feelings. Ask your uncle to read a passage at the ceremony; get your grandmother's advice (even if you decide to ignore it) about the dress, shoes, flowers, and so forth. If you make them feel important, included and loved, they will have a hard time holding on to their resistance. You just may find that by the time the wedding day has rolled around, your campaign of inclusion has successfully melted it away.

But as with your immediate families, don't let yourselves be manipulated with remarks such as "If you don't have a church wedding, it will kill your grandmother." Your grandmother is probably more resilient than anyone gives her credit for, and you should not succumb to her pressure—indeed, to anyone's—and compromise about an issue on which you feel strongly. There is no reason you can't say to your grandmother (or any other family member who is pressuring you): "Look, I know that the idea of a church wedding is important to you, but it's just not that important to us. What *is* important is your being there at the wedding, and I hope you can set aside your feelings for the day and join us."

□ *A House Divided*

Divorced parents create a special—and often especially painful—set of problems when you are planning a wedding. The fact that you are about to enter the very same institution that your parents have broken asunder is bound to be psychologically daunting. Moreover, divorced parents often present practical problems as well: Can each be invited without causing undue pain to the other? If you do invite both of them, won't it be awkward for you as well as for them? Can they be relied upon to behave? Some divorced couples can't bear to be in the same room with each other—what if your parents fall into this category?

But before you even begin to address the practical problems it is important that you understand the more subtle psychological ramifications of this situation. Here are some of the typical feelings that you, as a daughter of (or your fiancé as the son of) divorced parents are apt to be dealing with right now:

◆ As has been said earlier, there is often an unconscious wish to win your parents' love and approval when you tell them you are getting married. But the long-standing bitterness between your parents may prevent them from giving you the attention and positive reinforcement you want. They are apt to be much more involved in issues like "How *could* you ask your father to the wedding?" and "I don't want to see your mother again!" If this is the case, you are bound to feel disappointed and hurt.

◆ If your parents were divorced when you were a child, you may unconsciously still believe that you have some-how caused the breakup. When it comes time for you to marry, your wedding may provide the opportunity—at least on the fantasy level—of reuniting a broken family. Since that almost never is what happens, you are left with a great discrepancy between the unconscious wish for reunion and the present reality that offers no hope of it. This can lead to feelings of tremendous sadness and failure. If you are unable to bring your parents to-gether, it may well rekindle old feelings of loss and anger.

◆ If the friction between your parents is serious enough, you may find yourself in the position of acting like a parent to a pair of unruly children. Again, this will cause you to feel frustrated and angry, as you may rightly feel that the importance of your wedding is being usurped by their persistent quarreling. Also, your mother or father may unconsciously try to force you to choose a favorite (by insisting that you invite only her or only him), which only reinforces the unpleasant sense of role reversal.

◆ For parents who have alrady undergone the trauma of divorce, your upcoming marriage may be perceived as yet another break in an already fractured family. And because your marriage does represent a weakening of the parent/child bond, your wedding may reawaken their old feelings of loss. Yet another issue is that you may be your mother's last link to your father (and vice versa); when you marry, you are not only moving away from your parent, but you are also in a sense severing what may be the last remaining tie between your parents as well.

◆ Since all of the psychological factors described above are apt to make your parents feel their control over you is diminished, they are left feeling vulnerable and needy. As a result, they may go overboard in trying to exert their control over you, as a means of simply hanging on.

◆ Your mother is your strongest role model for how to behave in a male/female relationship. If your mother is divorced, then you are endowed with a less-solid foundation upon which to build your own marriage, which in turn may make you feel especially tense during the prewedding phase. You may also find yourself adopting the behavior of your mother as she moved through her unhappy marriage with your father; this scenario can come about for two main reasons. The first is that you may unconsciously want to test your fiancé's love for you. You may even want to drive him away—again, not on a conscious level at all—as a means of hastening what you feel is the inevitable conclusion to all such relationships: separation. The other reason you may try to assume your mother's role is to reenact your parents' marriage—only this time, the cast of characters has changed (yourself, your fiancé, etc.)—in order that the conclusion will be a happy one. You may have a powerful unconscious need to succeed where your parents failed.

What to Do

◆ Decide for *yourself* (and you may want to consult your fiancé and friends, as other family members are unlikely to be objective) whether or not you want both parents present. No one can—or indeed should—make this decision for you; only you know how you feel about your relationship with each of your parents. For example, at thirty, Miriam had not seen her father in more than twenty years and had no desire to invite him to her wedding. But for Peggy, who had remained close to her father despite his acrimonious parting from Peggy's mother, the idea of not inviting him to the wedding would have been terribly painful.

♦ Don't let parents place you in the middle of their conflict. Refuse to act as a messenger or go-between for them. If your father gives your mother instructions—via you—about how she is to behave on the wedding day, explain to him that you won't convey these instructions, and why. Instead, encourage your parents to express their own feelings to you, and be clear about expressing yours to them. DO NOT discuss one parent with the other, as you will only find yourself embroiled in their conflict.

♦ Enlist the aid and support of your fiancé when dealing with battling parents—they are less likely to cause a scene in front of your fiancé. Peggy has a mother who tends to loud displays of temper, particularly insofar as her ex-husband is concerned. But Peggy found that if she brought her fiancé along to dinner when she and her mother discussed wedding plans, her mother was less likely to make a scene. It was easier for Peggy to cope with her mother when she wasn't operating at top volume.

♦ Remind your parents that your wedding is for you, not for them, and encourage them to set aside their animosity for the day. You are not asking them to change their feelings, only to refrain from acting on them for a few hours.

□ *Resistance from Below*

Unlike many of the couples in this chapter, Helen and Keith didn't have any problems with their parents—the resistance they did have to face, however, was in the form of Helen's six-year-old son, Noah, and ten-year-old daughter, Julie, who resented the new man in their mom's life and did their best to show it. Helen's situation is hardly unusual; most women (and men) marrying for the second time find that their children are not at all happy—and this may be putting it mildly—about the idea.

If you are about to remarry, your children may well fear that they will be supplanted in your affections by your new mate; wedding preparations that take your time away from them may only intensify this apprehension. They may also feel defensive of the parent who is in a sense being "replaced" by the marriage: Your own children may feel the need to compare their own father to your new husband; his children will undoubtedly compare you to their mother.

You also need to understand that on some level, your children may still be hoping that you and their father will get back together. Your new marriage effectively puts an end to the buried wish that you and your former spouse will reconcile. So when your children express resistance to the new marriage, they may really be expressing their sadness at having to give up this fantasy.

Naturally, if your children from a previous marriage (or those of your fiancé) are resistant to the idea of the wedding, their bad feelings will engender a good deal of guilt in the two of you. But obviously, you are not going to cancel the wedding because of the kids; instead you have to find a way to draw them into the proceedings. The intense focus on the wedding may make it easy to overlook or ignore the concerns of your children, but this is exactly when they need to know, in a very concrete way, that your new marriage will not automatically exclude them. To accomplish that, use the prewedding period as an indication of things to come: If you include them in the planning, they won't feel shut out now or in the future.

What to Do

Insofar as possible, Helen and Keith encouraged the children to get involved in the wedding plans. There were, of course, many areas where their ages prevented participation, but here are a few ways in which they were able to pitch in:

◆ Since Helen's daughter, Julie, was in the wedding party, she was allowed to select the color of her dress (from a range of pinks that all the bridesmaids were considering). This gave her a sense that her opinions were important to her mother and also helped engender some excitement about the day when she would get to wear her pretty new dress.

◆ Both children went with Helen on lots of prewedding errands: florist, caterer, musicians, etc., which had the same emotional result: They felt included in the decision-making process and actually began to look forward to the wedding day.

◆ Helen's son, Noah, helped stick all the stamps onto the wedding invitations and went to the post office with his mother to mail them. Here, Noah actually felt that he was able to help his mother, which contributed to his own sense of importance and self-worth.

◆ Noah and Julie were allowed to invite one close friend each to the wedding. This meant that each child had an emotional ally on the big day, which helped prevent them from feeling excluded or overlooked in the excitement.

◆ Well beforehand, Helen made sure that the wedding photographer understood the importance of taking the childrens' pictures at the wedding. As a result, there are lots of pictures of the kids—both with Helen and Keith and without. Each child made his and her own keepsake "wedding album" after the ceremony.

◆ Before the wedding, Helen devoted an entire day to each child, in which they did something that intentionally was *not* wedding-oriented. With Noah, the day was spent going to the zoo and, later, roller skating; with Julie, the day consisted of a double feature at the movie theater and a trip to the mall for some new school clothes. In both instances, the time helped remind the children that their mother was still there for them, listening and responding to their needs.

□ *Final Note*

By getting married, you and your fiancé are changing the shape of both your families forever. Obviously, this joining of two lives—and all those to whom they are related—is among the most exalted moments of union in any life. Nonetheless, the power of such a coming together can also cause tremendous disruption; at the very least, there are going to be strong feelings expressed on all sides. What you need to keep in mind is that this is a time of transition—don't mistake the momentary resistance for ongoing opposition. Change—even at its most positive and joyous—requires significant readjustment.

4.

JEALOUSY:

The Green-Eyed Monster

◆

Trying to juggle the prewedding elation, anxiety, and resistance you are feeling takes plenty of psychological dex-
terity. But when you add the powerful emotion of
jealousy, you may begin to feel as though you just can't
keep up.

Part of the reason that jealousy is almost never discussed in terms of engagement and marriage is that it
seems so utterly contrary to the benevolent feelings you
anticipate. Nonetheless, it is one of the most commonly
felt prewedding emotions, and a refusal to acknowledge
jealous feelings—both your own and those of other people—can result in a good deal of damage to important
relationships caused by them as you move toward the
wedding itself.

□ *Identifying the Problem*

Interpersonal jealousy can take two major forms—the first is when you and/or your fiancé are jealous of the aspects of your lives that predate your relationship or exclude each other (friends, ex-lovers and -spouses, and even work). The second is the jealousy that your respective friends may feel when they are excluded by your decision to get married. In each case, you will need to hone in on the precise nature of the jealousy that you (or your fiancé, or friends) are feeling, so that you can minimize its impact on your relationship during the engagement period.

□ *Testing the Waters*

Partially out of need to test the new commitment that has just been made, you may find yourself inordinately jealous of your partner's ex-wife, former girlfriends, and even of his platonic female friends. Or you may find that he is experiencing this kind of jealousy toward your past.

Although the fact of your fiancé's previous relationships is unlikely to be news to you at this point, you may feel more threatened by his past now that you're about to become a wife, and vice versa.

This was especially true for twenty-seven-year-old Kitty, whose fiancé, Larry, was fourteen years her senior. Larry had also been married before, a fact of which Kitty was aware almost from the start of their relationship. "It had never bothered me before," she said, "but all of a sudden, when I heard any mention of his first wife, or even of his past girlfriends, I went nuts. It wasn't that I felt any real danger of losing him; after all, he had made the choice to be with me. No, it was an irrational feeling, like I couldn't bear to think he had been that intimate with someone who wasn't *me*."

Kitty has put her finger on an important point: More often than not, jealousy is not a simple matter of believing your partner is about to run off with someone else. Instead, it emerges from a much deeper feeling of wanting to be the "one and only" for your fiancé. While this feeling is perfectly understandable—and certainly common—it is also essentially an unrealistic one, because it hearkens back to the kind of relationship you wanted with your mother or father when you were a child. All children want to be daddy's best girl or mommy's favorite; getting married—with its promises of undying fidelity and devotion—may stir up these long-buried feelings. "I wasn't especially jealous before we got engaged," remarks Kitty, "but afterwards—watch out!" When Kitty was simply Larry's girlfriend, she didn't have the prerogative to feel jealous of his past—it was off-limits to her. And because of that, she was spared from thinking about what that past might mean to her. But once she and Larry became engaged, she began to feel that those prerogatives about his past did belong to her. With that feeling came an intensification of her jealousy and concern.

What to Do

Jealousy of this kind is not only painful, but it can also be debilitating to your relationship. Here are some things to keep in mind so that the Green-Eyed Monster doesn't get out of control:

◆ Separate fact from fantasy: Does he really see his ex-girlfriend all the time or is that an exaggeration on your part? Is she taking time away from your own relationship or is his contact with her confined to an annual Christmas card or lunch date?

◆ Remember that for some men, a looking at the past actually makes them more appreciative of the present. Says Larry: "Kitty got jealous when I wanted to have a drink with my former wife. But what she didn't realize is that though I enjoyed seeing Brenda, mostly I found myself thinking about all the ways in which she and Kitty were different, and I felt so lucky to have met Kitty!"

◆ Understand that your fiancé's attachment to his former lovers is actually a sign of emotional health and maturity. A man who has no contact with his past is shutting off major parts of himself, and in doing so, becomes less of a person. This is particularly true of his attachment to any children he may have from a former marriage. While it is all too easy to feel jealous of his son or daughter, you have to realize that the same devotion he displays toward them will undoubtedly be displayed toward any children the two of you go on to have. Encouraging him to cut himself off entirely from his former connections is a short-sighted and ultimately cruel tactic: You are in effect telling him to shirk his responsibilities (in the case of children) and to narrow his world.

◆ Accept that you don't have the right to deny your partner's past, and you wouldn't want to even if you could. His past is who he is; it has shaped him as completely and thoroughly as yours has you. What he has gained from former lovers and wives are part of the rich, complex human being you have chosen to marry, and he has probably learned some important lessons from them that will pass on as a legacy to you.

◆ Realize that in time your relationship with your fiancé will be severely debilitated if you insist on his cutting off all former ties. Not only will you be hurting him, but you will ultimately be hurting the valuable trust that you share.

◆ Insist that this relaxed and accepting attitude toward past relationships go both ways; you should feel equally free to see old boyfriends or a former husband—as long as these relationships in no way threaten your current one—for all the same reasons that he is entitled to revisit his past.

□ *Bosom Buddies*

Sometimes, the jealousy is not confined to past romances but also to friends. If you or your fiancé have any long-standing friendships with members of the opposite sex (relationships that are of a longer duration than that of you and your fiancé are even more difficult), there is plenty of room for jealousy to grow.

Jan's best friend, Ira, was also her business partner;

the two co-owned a small but thriving interior-design firm. When Jan told Ira that she and her boyfriend, Warren, were getting married, Ira immediately offered to "design" the wedding. Jan had always admired and respected his taste, and she eagerly shared his suggestions for centerpieces, floral décor, and the like with her fiancé. But Warren was less than charmed: "Maybe you and Ira should be getting married," he snapped. "The two of you certainly seem to agree on just about everything!" Jan realized with some surprise that her fiancé was jealous of her best friend, despite the fact that Ira was happily involved in a relationship of his own.

Even same-sex friends are not immune from your partner's jealousy, or your own. "Didn't you already see Jerry and Al three times this week?" complains Nicole to her fiancé. "Are you planning to have them move in after the wedding?"

"How many times a day do you two talk?" says Marvin when he finds his fiancé on the phone with her closest girlfriend. "Don't you ever get tired of each other?"

What to Do

Don't let unarticulated jealous feelings poison your prewedding planning or your marriage. Here are some ways of coping with your feelings—and his—to insure that they don't get out of hand:

◆ Try spending some brief time alone with your fiancé's friends, as a way of getting to know them. This can be very helpful, especially if you have been nagged by the feelings that his friends pose threats to your special relationship with him. By seeing them alone, you will help to diminish this symbolic power with which you have imbued them and gradually come to accept them for what they are: Other human beings who are important to and enrich the life of your beloved.

♦ Recognize that while you need to tolerate and get along with your partner's friends, you don't have to like them for themselves, or embrace them as your own. It is perfectly all right for him to enjoy the company of people who don't thrill you, and vice versa.

♦ Accept that your partner can (and indeed should) have friendships that don't include you, and that you are entitled to (and should exercise) the same privilege. A couple who have no one but each other will soon come to resent each other as symbols of their own isolation. No matter how much you adore your fiancé (and he adores you) no one can live comfortably with the love of only one other person. Everyone needs a number of close relationships in order to feel the proper sense of emotional nourishment. If you and your fiancé are too isolated, you will feel deprived and begin to blame each other for that sense of deprivation.

♦ Establish some ground rules for separate fraternizing now, before you get married. Agreeing to see friends alone during the week, but reserving Friday and Saturday nights for each other is one such arrangement you might make; establishing a curfew on phone calls, if you're living together (no calls after a certain hour when the two of you are home, unless there is an emergency) is another.

You may also find that you—or your fiancé—are deeply jealous of one another's attachment to other family members, particularly parents or siblings. Your fiancé may be jealous of your attachment to your father, or you may feel that he is too close to his mother. If you do suspect that such feelings exist, it's essential that you confront them directly. Jealousy of this kind has a particularly enduring quality that can make it poisonous to a relationship if it is ignored or buried.

◆

□ *Job Jealousy*

The jealousy that crops up during the prewedding period is not confined to other people and your various relationships to them. The jealousy can also be about something more concrete. A typical situation confronting many soon-to-be-marrieds is jealousy concerning careers, otherwise known as "job jealousy." Within the general category, there are basically two different kinds of job-related jealousy.

1. Either you or your fiancé has a very demanding job; the other one feels jealous of the time and energy that are necessary to expend to fulfill the stringent professional requirements of the job. Unless one of you has changed jobs recently, this is a situation that didn't begin when you got engaged. And yet it may be precisely because you *are* engaged—where the emphasis is on togetherness—that the time taken away from the relation-

ship is now a particular source of jealousy and annoyance.

Mitch is a salesman whose long hours and frequent business trips began to make his fiancée, Wendy, feel jealous and resentful as they got closer to the wedding day. "Sure I knew that his work was important to him, but I don't think that a job—any job—ought to take precedence over personal relationships." In order to compensate for his time away, Mitch began setting aside entire days—either weekends, holidays, or his vacation time—in which he and Wendy could be together. "Sometimes we did wedding-planning stuff, like order invitations or shop for his suit. But other times we just stayed at home with the VCR and plenty of freshly made popcorn."

Since workaholism is something that will affect a marriage as well as an engagement, Mitch and Wendy were emotionally savvy to devote some attention to it before the wedding, and you should take a lesson from them. Right now, it is especially important to make time to be together, even if you have to plan it into your busy calendars.

If possible, set aside a specific chunk of time—a Saturday morning, Sunday afternoon, Wednesday night—to just spend time together, without letting work intrude. By doing this, you are making a positive statement that the relationship needs more than the simply passive time when you are both home but involved in separate pursuits; it also requires time which you actively agree to spend together. And you will also be helping to minimize any jealousy you or your partner may be feeling about the pressures and demands of your respective work.

2. If there is a discrepancy in your jobs—one of you makes a great deal more money or has considerably more responsibilty—this can give rise to another kind of jealousy, more commonly known as plain old envy. Thirty-two-year-old Stephanie felt jealous because her own career in publishing seemed to be at a standstill. She had had the same job with no increase in responsibilities or authority for three years, while her fiancé, Zeke, had been promoted twice in an eighteen-month period. "I felt so mean-spirited being jealous of him, but I found I just couldn't help it," she says, her frustration obvious. "I so badly wanted for myself the kind of professional recognition he was getting."

For Penny, a New York–based art consultant, professional recognition and success came when she was able to clinch a big deal between an important corporate client and a prominent artist. "But in the midst of all these professional accolades," she recalls, "Albert felt jealous of my newfound success. He was at a professional low point and so I think my accomplishments were just making him feel even worse about himself."

Both couples—and indeed you and your partner if you are in this position—need to keep in mind the importance of being a team. Instead of focusing on what he/she has that you want, you must downplay the rivalry and instead focus on collective goals: a wonderful honeymoon, a summer home, a new car. One of the great joys of marriage is that self-interest becomes doubled. The team that is the two of you can accomplish things that might be impossible if you were alone.

This is as true emotionally as it is in a strictly material sense, and this feeling of well-being can carry over into your job. For instance, when Stephanie talked to Zeke about her jealousy, he said something that astonished her: He claimed that it was the stability of their relationship that had enabled him to make such terrific career strides in so short a time. Stephanie was both flattered and deeply touched by what he said, and began thinking about how she could channel some of that positive energy into her own situation at work.

When Albert was able to communicate his jealousy to Penny, she didn't focus on her own recent success. Instead, she talked to him about the slump that he was in, and together they hit upon some practical solutions for dealing with it. Once Albert had redirected his energy into the place it belonged—his own work—his jealousy about Penny's achievements subsided greatly. For Penny and Albert, as for Stephanie and Zeke, commitment to the relationship contributed to the furthering of their careers. Keep your eye on the finish line and remember that extraordinary things can happen—as long as you are rowing in the same direction.

☐ *A Special Case: The* Adam's Rib *Syndrome*

In the wonderful 1949 film *Adam's Rib,* Katharine Hepburn and Spencer Tracy play married lawyers who find themselves on opposite sides of a headline-making trial. What the professional rivalry does to their relationship is the point of the film, and by its end, they have both had to face some pretty deep truths about themselves and their marriage.

While the film was made more than forty years ago, the issues it raises may have even greater significance today. What about when you have a fiancé—soon to be husband—in the same profession? Will marriage intensify or resolve any professional jealousy that one or both of you might be feeling?

While no one can predict the future, there are a few caveats worth mentioning in this context. As thrilling as it may seem to share a career as well as a marriage— maybe you are both aspiring actors, architects—all too soon the cold, hard facts of promotion, competition, and compensation will take their toll on even the warmest of relationships. The decision you come to about this issue will not be easy, and so it is worthwhile giving it some consideration before the wedding. Nick and Alison, both thirty years old and graduates of the same law school class (not unlike Tracy and Hepburn!), wished that they had. Shortly after graduating, and only months before they decided to get married, they set up a fledgling law firm (along with another mutual friend from their class) in a small town in upstate New York. At first, things went along smoothly, but very soon they ran into trouble. Not only did Nick and Alison disagree on how several important new cases were to be handled, they found that each was turning to the third partner as a way of gaining an ally and settling their professional disputes. "And to make matters worse, there was just no relief from the situation," says Alison. "At five o'clock, we would close up shop and head home—together! Since we were already living together when we got engaged, there was no separation for either of us; we just took our nine-to-five troubles home, along with our briefcases."

Soon, professional disputes erupted into full-scale arguments, often with an unpleasantly personal tinge. "Nick would be criticizing the way I dealt with a client, and in the next breath, he was trying to draw parallels between how I dealt with the client and how I dealt with my father—it nearly drove me crazy!"

Things got so bad that the two decided to postpone the wedding for a while, until they could straighten out their professional troubles. "That's when it hit me," Alison recalls. "I understood that the professional stuff was getting in the way of our relationship and that it wasn't going to work. If things continued like this, I realized I would lose Nick and the firm would go down the tubes as well. It wasn't worth it."

Eventually, Alison was able to find a position with a larger firm in a town some miles from where she and Nick lived. And almost immediately domestic harmony was restored and plans for the wedding resumed. While neither Alison nor Nick wanted to give up being lawyers, they both agreed that finding different tracks within the same profession—and they both acknowledged that this took considerable thinking and planning ahead—is a highly recommended professional and personal strategy.

□ *Redefining Friendships*

Once you have told both of your families that you are getting married, you have successfully cleared one major prewedding hurdle. Telling your friends is usually the next major obstacle that most couples face.

Although it may take you unawares, friends, especially single ones, may feel jealous and possessive of you when you tell them you are getting married. This often comes as an unpleasant surprise—just at the moment when you expect them to exult in your good fortune, they may seem more than a bit out of sorts.

Single friends may resent—sometimes bitterly— your newly coupled status; they may be feeling that the friendship is bound to change, and that they will be excluded from your future plans and activities. Moreover, if being single is a source of pain to them, they may feel that your impending marriage is an implied condemnation (this is from their point of view, not yours) of being alone. Age plays a significant role here: If you are marrying in your twenties, your friends may be too immersed with finding jobs, starting careers, obtaining satisfactory living accommodations, to be threatened and jealous of your upcoming wedding. When you are twenty-four, the world and all its possibilities still feel wide open. But if you and your friends are in your thirties, and you're the one getting married, your wedding may have a very different meaning. "My best friend, Abby, tried so hard to be happy for me," said thirty-five-year-old Kim, "but the whole time I was making the wedding plans and asking her advice—

she was my maid of honor—I could just feel her thinking, 'This will never happen for me; I'm never going to find anyone.' Finally, she broke down and confessed all these awful feelings she had—how jealous she was, and how she wished that I had never gotten engaged. It hurt to hear some of those things, but in the end, it cleared the air and we could resume our friendship. I respect her for telling me; otherwise, the resentment would have gone on building and it might have ruined our relationship."

What to Do

♦ Arrange to spend some time with your friend—alone if possible or else with other friends—without your fiancé. Let your friends know that you still can and will function as a separate individual socially, despite the upcoming marriage.

♦ Be sensitive to friends' tolerance for hearing about the wedding plans. Don't feel you can't talk about it, but don't let that be the only topic of conversation between you, either. Make sure you ask her what's new in *her* life, how *her* job is going, and so forth.

♦ Remember to inquire about her romantic relationships, and give them your full time and attention. This may be easier said than done, especially if your friend is in a less-serious relationship than your own or none at all. Twenty-nine-year-old Vicky felt bored by listening to her friend Eileen's constant speculations about a man in her office on whom she had a crush. "It was like being in junior high school all over again," said Vicky. "She would eagerly report all these tiny snippets like, 'He was looking at me today,' and then ask 'Do you think he likes me?' It all sounded so immature." Vicky may be right, but she needs to understand that while her own relationship with her fiancé is far more advanced emotionally than her friend's present involvements, that is not a reason to disparage Eileen. And Vicky may not be aware that her relationship can actually serve as a model and an inspiration for Eileen. If you find yourself in similar circumstances, try to take your friend's relationship seriously, even if you find it seemingly juvenile. Think of yourself as a kind of teacher—in the best and gentlest sense of that word—and you may really be able to do some good.

◆ Consider making a small gift to a friend if she's feeling particularly left out or vulnerable. This needn't be a major purchase, but it should reflect your intimate knowledge of her tastes and likes: a great new knitting book for the friend who is handy with needles and yarn; pruning shears for the friend who has a passion for gardening; imported chocolates for the one with a sweet tooth.

◆ Accept that the friendship will change when you get married, and discuss this openly with your friend. To imagine that everything will be the same between the two of you is not only naive, but it will ultimately hurt the friendship by creating a false set of expectations that you will not be able to meet.

Ellen, an Atlanta-based textile designer, found this out the hard way. She was determined not to let her long-time friend Kate feel left out when she and her boyfriend of two years decided to get married, so she invited Kate to go on vacation with them. The three spent two awkward weeks traveling along the California coast, the tension between them mounting every day. "At night, when Joel and I went to our room, I could feel her silent reproaches seeping through the walls. We had been such good companions for so long; now she thought I was a deserter. During the day, she could barely contain her resentment toward Joel. It was an awful trip; now I can see that the idea was doomed from the start. You know what they say about two being company, and three being a crowd . . ."

What Ellen was trying to avoid was the fact that friendships do change drastically after marriage, but this needn't spell their demise. The goal is to maintain as much about the friendship as possible while at the same time openly acknowledging that you are no longer as available to your friend.

"Kate and I had to go through a long cooling-off period," says Ellen. "She was used to being able to drop by without phoning, and to calling late at night when she knew I was up. And of course, all the traveling she and I did together when we were both unattached . . . there were a lot of new things we both had to adjust to, and for a while, she felt kind of distant from me. But we kept talking about it, and gradually, she was able to accept the changes. In a way, I think that being able to weather this has made us even closer than before."

□ *The Three Musketeers Phenomenon*

An interesting offshot of the jealousy problem between friends might easily be called The Three Musketeers syndrome, though it can apply to larger groups of friends as well.

As you probably know from experience, closely knit groups of friends are common to the single life. You depend on your friends—and they on you—for both practical and emotional sustenance. Sharing a summer house, regular get-togethers, and intense daily phone conversations are all part of this state of bachelorhood, for members of either sex. Trudy, Beth and Marian were a perfect example. They indulged in lengthy phone conversations almost daily, coordinated their summer vacations so they could take trips together, met weekly for dinner and a movie and monthly for a shopping spree at the local malls and discount centers. Nothing could separate the three women—that is, until Beth got engaged to Roy. Suddenly, it seemed like the group had fallen apart and Trudy and Marian were left feeling jealous and miserable.

This story is not uncommon. As wonderful as all of your camaraderie is, it usually comes to an end when a member of the group decides to get married. The other friends in your group are apt to feel jealous and deserted when you announce your engagement, because they know that a new bond will inevitably tear you away from them.

Yet what can often happen is that group members

are so finely attuned to one another's emotional states that sometimes a chain reaction is set off by your impending wedding. Kelly, a twenty-nine-year-old nurse from Boston, found that this was the case with her fiancé's close friends. At first, George's two best friends ribbed him constantly about getting married. "That's the end of the romance," kidded Hal. "It's all dirty dishes and hair rollers from now on!" And Vince, the other member of this little enclave, added, "She's really got you under her thumb now; she's never going to let you out alone again."

Kelly was understandably distressed by their reaction, but instead of just flying off the handle, she tried to see the situation from their point of view. The three men had gone to college together, been in the same fraternity, and played on the same teams. Now, they co-owned a sailboat together, and Vince even worked at the same computer-graphics firm that George did. Naturally, they viewed Kelly as an intruder, and they expressed their apprehension about losing George by their ceaseless teasing.

But what Kelly didn't expect was the powerful impact that George's decision would have on his two closest buddies. Within two months of learning of Kelly and George's engagement, Vince declared that he was going to marry the woman he had been seeing for the past year and a half. And suddenly, just three months after that and almost on the eve of Kelly's wedding to George, Hal announced that he was head over heels in love and about to tie the knot himself. "It's like they were programmed or something," she said, laughingly, recounting the alacrity with which Hal and Vince decided to get married. "Once they had accepted the idea that they couldn't kid George out of his choice, they did a complete turnabout," she adds. "George began to tease *them* about making it a triple ceremony, since they had jumped on the bandwagon so quickly."

So don't be surprised if your wedding inspires your closest chums—and his—to follow suit. Weddings are powerfully emotional turning points, and the idea can shake up a whole group, encouraging more than one member of it to solidify his or her own relationship. Often, the particular bond between friends is so strong that once it is broken, it will disrupt the emotional balance in a way that can't be mended. Instead, members of the group will unconsciously seek out new alliances—i.e., marriages of their own.

The Three Musketeers syndrome actually has some nice side effects, too, because it means that you and your friends (or your fiancé and his) can now commiserate with people who are going through the same set of emotional experiences that you are. You may find that your group has reconstituted itself in a new way, and that the same friends who accompanied you on your search for the perfect black cocktail dress are now sharing the search for the perfect white one.

□ *Final Note: A Plea for Jealousy*

Jealousy has always had a pretty bad reputation: A close cousin to envy, it is considered childish and morally wrong, a character flaw that needs to be overcome. And to a large extent, this is true: Out of control, jealousy will cause terrible trouble between you and your fiancé.

But having said all that, it must be pointed out that there is also a positive side to this much-maligned human emotion. Not only is it a perfectly natural feeling, in small doses, jealousy can be flattering and even desirable. After all, jealousy is an index of the intensity of our feelings. When someone doesn't matter much, it is rare that you feel the pangs of jealousy. While if you are mildly jealous of your fiancé, he may feel a touch of annoyance, but deep down, he is probably a little pleased, too: your jealousy demonstrates the depth and power of your feeling for him. And the same is true when he feels jealous of you. But remember, jealousy is like a very strong seasoning: A little goes a long way and too much will ruin the meal entirely.

5.

MISTRUST:

Living in the Material World

•

You're already familiar with a number of powerful emotions: anxiety and elation, jealousy and resistance. But now you may find yourself increasingly concerned with more concrete issues—such as money and your future home—that would have previously seemed unrelated to your emotional life.

Yet you probably also are coming to understand that these—and indeed all—material issues are directly connected to some deeper emotive state. Unconscious feelings raised by such issues can catch you unawares. It is easy to quarrel long and hard about his careless spending habits, or your excessive neatness, without fully understanding that you are really battling over issues of trust in your relationship.

□ *Mutual Funds*

Money—and how it is handled—is a powerful signifier of trust in a marriage. Time and time again, disagreement about money is cited in divorce hearings as one of the foremost reasons for failed marriages. Although it is certainly true that the very real exigencies of finances can cause marital problems, at the heart of the money issue is the far more important issue of trust. It is therefore essential that you and your fiancé give some thought now, before you get married, to the issue of trust and how it is expressed through money.

□ *Caveat Emptor*

The economic watchwords for prospective brides—and grooms—in the coming decade are: the Prenuptial Agreement. In order to make an informed emotional choice about so significant an issue, you must first understand what a prenuptial agreement entails and why it is sought. A prenuptial agreement, which is usually prepared by an attorney, is basically a financial agreement made in anticipation of the marriage. Under the terms of this agreement, both parties contractually bind themselves to waive any rights to inherit or lay claim to property belonging to the other in the event of divorce or death. If a dispute should arise at some future time, the prenuptial agreement is legally enforceable in a court of law.

This represents a radical break with tradition. In decades past, it was not uncommon for a bride to relinquish all financial claims as a sign of her devotion (feminine self-abnegation being an equivalent for an expression of true love). But now, largely as a result of the femininist movement (which has meant that women have become increasingly aware—and protective—of all their rights, including financial ones) such an arrangement no longer seems to make sense. Rather than thinking of the pre-nuptial agreement as a sign of distrust—as some have construed it to be—women and men have *both* come to understand that it is instead a symbol of trust *shared*.

Furthermore, the high rate of divorce has unfortu-nately made marriage less of a lifetime institution than a temporary alliance. And if you or your fiancé has been married before, this is even more of an issue: You have reason to be cautious, because you have prior experience that justifies being cautious. Couples with children from previous marriages also have good reason to sign pre-nuptial agreements; otherwise, in the event of a divorce or death, your children could end up the losers.

While the decision to sign a prenuptial agreement is a highly personal one, here are two stories that illustrate some of the pros and cons of the issue.

STORY ONE: *"Her Daughter's Keeper"*
Thirty-six-year-old Claudia—about to embark on her sec-ond marriage to thirty-seven-year-old William—describes her reasons for insisting on a prenuptial agreement this way: "Since I have a ten-year-old daughter from my first marriage, I wanted to make sure that she would be pro-tected no matter what happened between William and

me. I had made a good bit of money on a very smart real estate investment, and I was determined to set it aside for her college education. My attorney advised me that in the event of a divorce, not only could William attempt to claim that money, but if he filed a suit, the money would be tied up until the suit was settled. But meanwhile, how would my daughter, Laura, finance her education?

"So I had my attorney draw up a prenuptial agreement in which William, by signing, relinquished all claims to that money. I love William and I think we're really going to make it together, but at the same time, I have to protect Laura's future—I'm responsible for her after all."

STORY TWO: *"Risks and Rewards"*

For Amanda, who stood to inherit a large fortune from her wealthy family, opting not to sign a prenuptial agreement was actually a sign of emotional liberation from parents who had long used their money as a means of exerting emotional control over their children. According to Amanda, hers is an emotionally remote family in which money is the only tangible symbol of affection. At the same time, however, her family discouraged her and her sister from developing any close emotional ties with anyone outside the family. "My parents always cautioned me against being generous to friends," she says. "They were very concerned that I would be taken advantage of because of my money." When Amanda and Charles got engaged, her parents urged her to have a prenuptial agreement drawn up immediately. "Not only did they want to protect my inheritance from *any* claim that Charles might conceivably make, they wanted me to put the house we had bought and were renovating in my name only. Their rationale for this was the fact that it was my money which was paying for the work on the house. He was an outsider; someone not to be trusted yet—if ever."

At first, Amanda was tempted to go along with what her parents suggested. But Charles put his foot down. He said that as much as he loved and trusted Amanda, she could not ask him to live in a house that was not technically his. As they thrashed the problem out—and the fight was a bitter one—Amanda began to realize that the whole issue of the prenuptial agreement was no more than a continuation of the control her parents had always tried to exert with their wealth, and she no longer wanted any part of it. "Of course, I know it's a risk," she says of her decision not to ask for a prenuptial agreement, "but everything is a risk—not the least of which is the marriage itself—and I feel this is a risk worth taking. Charles is also part of my family. His needs are as important to me as those of my parents. At long last, I'm beginning to put these things in proper perspective and get some handle on them."

All this somewhat sobering information should not shake your trust in your fiancé. However, it is true that an honest assessment of what each partner brings to the marriage in financial terms can only enhance the trust that you share.

There is really no clear cut right or wrong answer here. You and your fiancé will have to decide what is right for you. To help in reaching that decision, consider the issue from a clinical perspective.

While I understand the reasons why the prenuptial agreement has gained favor, I nonetheless see it as a way of injecting an element of distrust into the relationship at precisely the moment when trust is what is most needed. A prenuptial agreement may actually create the very feeling you are trying to guard against.

Although it may be a perfectly rational way of protecting property, I still think the prenuptial agreement represents only an illusory form of safety. No agreement can protect you against disappointment, infidelity, betrayal, or all the other things that people really worry about when they are about to get married. In fact, prenuptial agreements may be a way of giving in to the mistrust, rather than overcoming it. If you don't begin your marriage with a trusting heart, then your marriage is at a disadvantage from the outset. In a way, you are unconsciously siding with the possibility of divorce and, in a sense, anticipating it.

Let me dramatize my point this way: My wife and I had a baby-sitter to look after our daughter. On one occasion, the baby-sitter asked to borrow a small sum of money, which we loaned to her; on another, she asked to borrow our car and we again said yes. She expressed some surprise at how easily and willingly we trusted her with our belongings. To which we replied: 'We trust you

*with our child—how could we possibly not trust you with
some money or our car?' I think the issue is the same. If
you trust someone enough to marry, to merge your life
with, and create a new family with, then what does it
mean to place limitations on this trust when it comes to
your material possessions? Insisting upon a prenuptial
agreement seems to me to be raising questions about
trusting your partner right from the beginning."*

◆

□ *We're in the Money*

Prenuptial agreements are only one—though perhaps the
most obvious—of the ways in which you can help to make
rational the complex issues of money and trust. But there
are many other money related questions that you will
need to ask yourselves, and many other emotional issues
that will surface in the process. Here are a number of
those that you ought to be asking each other and yourselves now, before you get married:

1. *Do you plan to maintain one bank account or
two?* This can be a touchy subject, especially if you are
used to handling your own money and not having to
answer to anyone else about your purchasing decisions.
"I'm too old to discuss how much I've paid for a pair of
shoes with *anyone*," says thirty-five-year-old Celeste, a
pharmacist, "and I'm not about to start now." Many couples opt for a yours-mine-and-ours sort of arrangement,
in which three (or more) separate accounts are main-

tained. Each partner continues to pay for expenses that are exclusively hers or his, while joint expenditures—rent or mortgage payments, vacation, car—come out of a joint account held just for that purpose. Paychecks are deposited into a joint account, from which you can then transfer funds to your individual accounts. Of course, this arrangement presupposes that both of you are working and bringing in an income. But even if there is only one wage earner between you, you might still want to consider individual accounts for personal spending. As the women's movement has taught us, a woman who stays at home is nevertheless a significant contributor to the maintenance and functioning of a household, a position that should be reflected in how finances are organized.

2. *Will credit cards be maintained separately or jointly?* As with the issue of bank accounts, sharing credit cards ultimately does mean that you have to answer to—or at least discuss—your spending habits. Now, while it is reasonable to assume that as a married couple you will be doing that anyway, many women (and men, too) prefer to maintain a degree of autonomy about their charge accounts. This is especially true if you have been earning and handling your own money for a while. You can also consider the "yours-mine-ours" alternative described above, where each of you maintains separate cards for individual purchases and one (or more) joint account for shared expenses—restaurants, travel, home furnishings, and the like.

3. *How will household expenses be shared?* The obvious choice is simply to split the costs evenly, but this may be unrealistic, especially if there is a discrepancy between your salary and that of your fiancé. Sometimes, one of you may feel uncomfortable with a life-style that is beyond your means. "Steve wanted us to live in this very fancy neighborhood that I never could have afforded on my salary," says twenty-nine-year-old Fran, who works in a day-care center. "I know a lot of women would be thrilled, but I've always been used to paying my own way and it's hard to change that now." Or if yours is the greater income, your fiancé may feel even more uneasy about not pulling his financial weight, because he believes men are still expected to be the bigger wage earners. But as has been emphasized earlier, to get beyond this issue, you have to focus on the team that is the two of you. One of you may earn more money, but that doesn't mean that the other is not making significant contributions—both monetary and otherwise—to the relationship.

4. *Do you plan to make each other the beneficiary (to any life insurance policies, etc.) or heir (in the event that you have already drawn up wills)?* Although a future husband or wife certainly seems like the obvious choice here, if one or both of you have children, some provision will naturally have to be made for them. Also you may have a very close friend or another relative whom you want named in your will or as a cobeneficiary; the same can be true for your fiancé. Discussing such issues during the engagement period is a good idea, because you may have very different ideas about how these matters should be handled and it is worthwhile ironing out any differences early on.

5. *If one or both of you already have valuable material possessions—stocks, bonds, house or apartment, land, car—will the ownership be made joint?* This is a loaded issue, which should be considered seriously before any hasty decisions are made. With something that is used by both of you—a house or car, for example—there are very good reasons why the ownership should be joint. Take the case of Amanda and Charles, cited earlier in this chapter. Charles didn't want to live in any home that wasn't his, and this is a reasonable reservation. But in the case of Claudia and William, the money she had received from the sale of her property was earmarked for a particular purpose—her daughter's education—and so joint ownership of this money was not the right choice.

6. *If one or both of you have children, how will the expenses for their care be divided up?* The answer to this question could cause serious friction later on, so it's worth thinking—and talking—about now. Will your fiancé resent any expenses that come from caring for any children from your former marriage? Will you resent any financial obligation he has to his children, and even, perhaps, to his ex-wife? Encourage each other to be frank and *specific* in your discussions. For instance, your fiancé might not object to helping foot the bill for your son's food and clothing, but he might well resent having to pay for an expensive private school. To keep the peace, you may want to consider paying for it yourself or asking your ex-husband to pitch in. Or you might be annoyed by the huge phone bills his teenage daughter runs up during her visits and the abandon with which she uses her father's—and what may soon be your—credit cards. In this case, your fiancé may need to have a heart-to-heart talk with her, in which a few limits are set.

7. *How do the decisions about money get made between you now?* Is this satisfactory to both of you? If not, can you think of ways to change it? Couples that argue about money may well be expressing their lack of trust and confidence in each other. "Money is almost more intimate than sex," quips Regina, a twenty-four-year-old sales-marketing representative. "I slept with my fiancé long before I trusted him with my checkbook!" Since money and how it gets used is an issue that will last all your married life, it is essential to address it now. If you find that you and your fiancé tend to quarrel about money now—he criticizes your shopping habits, you think he's miserly when it comes to gift-giving—stop and ask yourself if you're not using money as a symbol to mask some other feeling of displeasure and annoyance.

For instance, what you consider his less-than-generous attitude toward gifts may be your way of saying that you need more demonstrations of his love. Conversely, in criticizing your shopping habits, your fiancé may be trying to tell you that you're devoting too much attention to things outside the relationship, with the result that he feels deprived. But if it really comes down to a fundamental difference in the way you perceive money—you're a saver, he's spender—you will need to find some form of compromise early on.

Note: Because money is such a potential hot spot, which can evoke such powerful feelings of mistrust between you, understand that the decisions you make don't have to be acted upon right away. For instance, you and your fiancé may decide to keep your finances separate for several months before, and even after, the wedding. Many couples decide to maintain separate bank accounts until well after the wedding. It is only later, when many other prewedding tensions have subsided, that they pool all their monies and other resources.

□ *Your Greatest Asset: Your Health*

In the past, the engagement period was a time to examine not only the financial status of the prospective bride and/ or groom, but their health—both physical and mental—as well: Were there any diseases that ran in the family that could be passed along to future generations? What about the couple themselves—were they each free from any serious or potentially debilitating illnesses?

While ten years ago such questions may have seemed antiquated and outmoded, the terrible reality of AIDS and other sexually transmitted diseases has suddenly made them pertinent once again. Presumably, you and your fiancé already know whatever is necessary to know about one another's past sexual histories. But if you have any concern whatsoever about the possibility of contracting a sexually transmitted disease, then you and your partner should be tested, and the engagement period is the appropriate time for such testing to take place.

□ *Home Is Where the Heart Is*

Another big issue of trust between you and your fiancé can easily be symbolized by where you and he are going to live. If you have both decided to abandon your "bachelor digs" and look for a new place to live, you can consider yourselves lucky. You will have the luxury of choosing a new home that adequately addresses both your needs and tastes.

But if you're like most Americans—and city dwellers get the worst of it here—finding a new and larger place to live may be beyond your financial capabilities right now, or at any time soon. If that is so, you will have to make what has now become the classic choice: "Your place or mine?" Athough you may not realize it at first, these four little words constitute another major emotional decision, around which feelings of mistrust and doubt may well come to a head.

Obviously, there are only two versions of this story: Your fiancé moves in with you, or you abandon your place and move in with him. Here's how these scenarios generally get played out between you:

SCENARIO ONE: *The Invasion of the Identity Snatcher.*
This is the scenario in which your fiancé moves in with
you. Although you clearly love him and want to be with
him, you may nevertheless feel as if an unwelcome intruder has invaded your own personal space. "He had all
these heavy old oak pieces—a dresser, a dining room
table, an armoire, a bunch of chairs—that had belonged
to his grandmother," wails Terry, whose fiancé moved
into her garden apartment when his own lease expired,
shortly before the wedding. "I felt like my good-sized
two-bedroom place—which had always seemed so spa-
cious for me—had suddenly become an antique furniture
warehouse!"

Lack of space is only one problem; the loss of privacy
and differences in taste are two of the more-common
ones you may have. "I just wasn't used to someone else
being there all the time," said Jody, a thirty-one-year-old
with a successful dog-grooming business. "Talking on the
phone; smearing a green-clay mask all over my face; turning up my favorite music really loud—these were all
things I was used to enjoying *alone*. When Alex moved
in, I felt like I had ceased to be myself somehow; I was
tiptoeing around my own place and I didn't like it." Jody
also found that her preference for a clean, uncluttered
modern look was not shared by her fiancé. "He collects
everything—stamps, coins, shells, polished rocks, butter-
flies under glass. Not only does that stuff take up room,
but he wanted to display it all over the place!"

Terry adds this complaint: "The worst thing—and
I'm a little embarrassed to admit it—is his cat. I like

animals as well as the next person, and when Derek asked if I could stand living with his sixteen-year-old obese striped cat, I said all right. But when he moved in, it was clear that the animal hated me! He hisses when I come near him, won't eat the food I put out for him, and generally lets me know that he totally disdains me. When I've pointed this out to Derek, he says that the cat's just nervous from having moved so recently. But what about me? I feel as though I've got two new house guests and one of them can't even be civil to me!"

SCENARIO TWO: *Estrangement in Paradise*

The other side of this coin is when you give up your place and move in with your fiancé. In this case, you're obviously not going to feel invaded, although you and your partner may still have clashes about differing tastes, need for privacy, and lack of adequate space.

But leaving a place of your own to move in with someone else—even someone you love—may cause you to feel alienated and displaced, much like a stranger in the very place that is supposed to be home.

"I didn't have any place in Conrad's house that was exclusively mine," says Marsha, who moved into the small Los Angeles bungalow her fiancé had lived in for the last seven years. "He had been living there long enough to have gotten pretty firmly settled in, and it felt as if there wasn't any room for me—my things, my hobbies, my taste. His Navajo rugs were all over the walls and floors; his collection of Mexican pottery lined the shelves. The furniture, pictures—pretty much everything, in fact—had been arranged just the way he liked it, and I was reluctant to suggest changing a thing."

But even if your fiancé hasn't created the "perfect" environment, you may still find it difficult to move into the place that has been his alone. "Although Jeremy had been living in his apartment for three years, it looked like he had never finished unpacking," says Claire of her fiancé's Brooklyn apartment. "There were still things in boxes, the walls were just about bare, and his mattress—without the box spring—was sitting on the floor. And yet he seemed to like things the way they were and had a hard time when I put up a new shower curtain or bought a new tablecloth for the kitchen."

Nor is the sense of displacement you are likely to feel exclusively centered around the physical space and how your fiancé has filled it. Sometimes, the sense of alienation comes from how the two of you function within a space that was once exclusively his.

"When I moved into Albert's apartment, I wasn't at all bothered by issues of taste and aesthetics," says Penny, who was quoted earlier in chapter 4. "Albert has a fantastic eye and I'd always thought his place looked great. When I moved in, we were able to incorporate some of my favorite things—an English secretary that had belonged to my godmother, a brass bird cage I had found at a garage sale—into his design scheme, and we both agreed the place looked even better than before." So what was the problem? "It had more to do with Albert's friends, who were used to dropping over three and four times a week, without even phoning first. Albert's place was so attractive and comfortable that it became *the* spot where all his cronies congregated. It's not that I didn't like his friends, but I didn't like them in our place all the time. It made me feel that I constantly had to be a hostess and I just couldn't relax. I got cast as the interloper in this situation; before, the door had always been open, and now I had come in and started to close it."

What to Do

Here are a number of concrete methods you can use to improve a living situation that is less than ideal:

♦ Within the house or apartment, try to establish some areas that belong exclusively to each of you. While you may not have the luxury of an entire room, don't overlook closets (that can, with the aid of a table top and chair, become a mini work area or study) or corners that can be outfitted with desk and lamp, or even your (or his) own favorite armchair and foot rest.

♦ Try, within the limits of your budget, to make a few redecorating decisions together. Maybe you can stand the furniture but find the rug intolerable; suggest a shared outing to go shopping for a new one together. One or two furniture purchases, a few decorative objects or a new shade of paint—all agreed upon by both of you— can go a long way toward making both of you feel that the place you're living in is really home.

♦ Make a list—and have your fiancé do the same—indicating domestic arrangements you require, things you can't abide, and things about which you are willing to negotiate. Penny's list of "must haves" included a greater degree of "alone time" in their shared space, dishes to be washed right after dinner, and late-night soaks in the tub; Albert's list of things he couldn't stand included pantyhose and underwear dangling from the shower curtain rod, music played too loudly, and failing to clean out the tub after the late-night baths.

♦ Arrange to spend some time away from the house or apartment, in order to allow your partner some time there alone. You can use this time to see friends, go to a gym or health club, pursue an independent hobby, catch up on some work at the office, see a film, or experience some other cultural event your fiancé doesn't enjoy. By all means tell him what you have decided to do, and discuss his willingness to grant you the same kind of private time at home.

□ *Final Note*

Don't let material possessions—money, home, furniture, car—mask the real issues of trust in your relationship with your partner. In your discussions and in dealing with these issues, keep in mind that it is all too easy to think the objects themselves are the source of the conflict. Any time you have a disagreement about one of these subjects, keep asking yourself, "How does this relate to the feelings of trust—or lack of them—in our relationship?" It may take you a while to come up with any answers, but the reiteration of the question will put you back on track.

6.

FEAR:

Will Marriage Change Us Forever?

◆

As the wedding day draws closer, you may well find that your anxieties have started to escalate into full-scale fears. But these fears are more than simply an intensification of your anxieties; they also possess a distinct character all their own. While your earlier anxieties were an immediate response to the decision to get married, the fears you are encountering now are probably concerned with deeper, more-resonant emotional issues. And while many common anxieties have to do with your relationship to your beloved—and how marriage will change it—your fears may have more to do with your sense of yourself as an individual and your relationship to the world at large.

In response to the fear of change that many couples express, I would go so far as to say that marriage is supposed to change you. It won't make you into a new person, or solve all your problems, but marriage is a major life event that should precipitate growth, development, and yes, change in the individual. Rather than something to be feared, I see these changes as something to be welcomed; *it means that your relationship is not static, but instead, constantly evolving.*

Yet I have also noticed that many people have highly unrealistic expectations about how marriage will change them. They believe that marriage is a magic ritual that can transform their lives and solve all their emotional problems. Unfortunately, this is not true. Sadly enough, marriage won't change some people at all. For those people, marriage is simply a new attempt at solving old problems.

◆

□ *Good-bye to All That*

As has been said earlier, marriage emphatically marks the end of your childhood. But in the midst of your elation, you dealt with the *positive* aspects of that statement: the happiness that comes with truly feeling like an autonomous adult. Now you must accept that the same statement is also a cause for apprehension.

In the past, your relationship to your parents was that of an individual child relating to a married unit. But now that *you* are about to enter into the state of matrimony, you can no longer rely on this way of relating to your parents. Instead, you will be approaching them as a married woman; your marriage creates a greater sense of equality between you and your parents. While that can be liberating, it can also be frightening in that it subtly diminishes the comforting authority your parents may have had in your mind.

"I was so used to thinking that my mother knew everything, just because she had been married all those years," says twenty-four-year-old Anna. "I trusted her experience about things. But now that I'm getting married myself . . ." she trails off and thinks for a moment. "I'm starting to look very critically at her marriage to my dad and I've been noticing a lot of things about it that I don't like. It hurts a little to think these things about her; I've always considered her to be so perfect."

□ *Mixed Doubles*

The fear of losing the link to your childhood that this new equality with your parents represents is only one of the myriad fears that are likely to emerge during this period. You may also unconsciously be harboring the fear that by getting married, you will inevitably end up just like your parents. If you understand that a large part of growing up has been the struggle to define yourself in contradistinction to your parents, what does it mean to be entering precisely the same relationship that they occupied in your childhood? After all, the most important single model for male/female relationships that you have is the one established by your parents all those years ago. It is inevitable that you are going to be thinking about *their* relationship to one another and how that affected you.

If your parents have had a good relationship, you may, without knowing or understanding it, feel competitive and harbor doubts about your ability to live up to it. "My parents were always so wrapped up in each other, my sisters and I often felt left out," says twenty-five-year-old Mary Kaye, an accountant from Philadelphia. "They seemed to have this storybook romance, and we kids felt outside of it." In speculating on her own wedding, she adds, "I know that Tom and I have a different kind of relationship than my parents did. In all my years growing up, I never heard them raise their voices to one another, whereas Tom and I can really go at it sometimes. I hope that doesn't mean we're really not made for each other." It is also possible that you will feel threatened by the example set by one of your parents. "It was a little strange telling my mother that Harvey and I were getting married," says twenty-nine-year-old Meryl. "I half expected her to tell me that I was too young. I guess I'm so accustomed to thinking of my mother as a person who can do anything—she's a terrific cook, successful businesswoman, funny, good-looking, and smart. Since I don't feel nearly as competent, I found myself thinking, 'How can I be anyone's wife?' I somehow imagined that when I was ready to get married I would magically become the person she was. Well, that hasn't happened."

Your parents may have had a decent but far-from-perfect relationship, and you can easily worry that the same low-level domestic discord you watched as a child will be yours as a married woman. "I know my folks really do love each other a lot," says thirty-two-year-old Denise, a high school teacher in Dallas, "but my mother is just such a confirmed nag—she's always after my dad for one thing or another. Sometimes it's a big issue, like why he doesn't make more money or why he isn't more aggressive in his business. But I've seen her get crazy over little things, too; for instance, if he forgets to pick something up at the store when he's promised. I don't ever want to behave that way, and yet I can be such a perfectionist myself at times that I worry I'm going to turn out just like her." And if the relationship between your parents was so bad that it ended in divorce, then you will have a very special set of fears—described in chapter 3—with which to contend.

Before the engagement, you and your fiancé probably unconsciously believed that anything was possible. Your relationship was a clean slate on which you were free to inscribe anything you wished. Now that you're engaged and looking ahead to marriage, you are no longer in an unprecedented relationship. The model— for better or worse—is your parents, and the recognition of these limits may cause you to feel distressed.

□ *Going It Alone*

One of the other great fears of the prewedding period is caused by the imminent surrender of your single status.

The older you are, the more you are apt to feel frightened by the thought of giving up what may well have been a satisfying and successful (if sometimes lonely) single life. There is a tremendous vitality that is gained by trying—and succeeding—in forging a life for yourself. When you opt to marry, you give all that up—for good reasons, of course—but the renunciation of that life is nevertheless bound to make you fearful. Consider the questions below as a way of probing what may be your hidden fears about renouncing your life as a single woman (or man):

Testing Your Hidden Fears

1. Have you lived alone for more than five years?

2. Are you satisfied with your choice of profession? Does your work continue to stimulate and engage you?

3. Do you have a satisfying and varied social life?

4. Have you made significant life decisions—about a job, professional school, or a move to another city or town—on your own?

5. Are you financially self-sufficient?

6. Do you enjoy spending time, even traveling, by yourself?

7. Are you a person for whom a particular routine is important? Do you become annoyed or irritable if that routine is disrupted?

8. Are you very rigid about matters of personal taste in home décor, clothing, and the like? Do you find it hard to imagine ever compromising on an issue of taste to accommodate someone else?

If you have answered "yes" to most of these questions, then it is likely that you will be experiencing (even if not consciously) some various fears about the dissolution of your solitary state, which marriage will perforce bring about. Says thirty-nine-year-old Deborah: "My long training to become a veterinarian and the demanding work I do has made me feel proud of myself, both as a woman and as an individual. It's not that I don't want to get married—I do, very much—but I still feel a little sad and even frightened about giving up the sense of singleness that has sustained me for so long." And Tina, a thirty-one-year-old violinist with a large orchestra, adds this: "I had a full and satisfying life before I got engaged; I did a lot of traveling, both alone and with friends, and my work is a constant joy to me. I'm used to doing things alone and for myself, and I've liked that. I don't want to become dull, predictable, and boring. Yet part of me is still feeling the thrill of being engaged—the whole thing is just very confusing." And finally, Gwen, a thirty-three-year-old stockbroker who has not lived with her fiancé (or anyone else), says: "I've been on my own for so long now—I'm afraid I just can't change to get along with anyone on a day-to-day basis!"

You may also feel afraid that the independence that attracted your mate in the first place will vanish as a result of your marriage. "I know that Kevin has always made a big deal of what he calls my 'feistiness,' " says thirty-two-year-old Maureen, who works as an undercover police agent. "He thinks I have a lot of spunk, and I guess I do. You certainly need it in my profession. But now that I'm getting married, I wonder if I'll lose some of that appeal for him."

Related to this is the fear that your hard-won independence has really been no more than a temporary situation and that once married, you will grow dependent and clinging. "I don't especially like living alone," says thirty-five-year-old Audrey, who designs sportswear for a major women's-clothing company, "but I've always done it, and over the years I've gotten kind of proud at how well I can deal with the cranky landlord and put the mousetraps out by myself. I'm just afraid that once we get married, I'm going to turn into this stereotypical helpless female."

On the other hand, if you answered no to the majority of these questions, you may well be experiencing a set of fears of a quite different but no-less-troubling kind: that of being engulfed by marriage before you have had a chance to really become your own person. This is especially true if you are young and have had limited experience with men and in the world. Says Heather, a twenty-two-year-old from Florida whose college graduation coincided with her engagement: "In a way, I was lucky. Eric and I have been going together since our freshman year. I'm crazy about him, and I really always have been. We have a good relationship: supportive, solid, caring, and fun. When he proposed—two weeks before graduation—I was so happy. I think if I looked for the next twenty years, I wouldn't find anyone I loved or wanted to be with more. And yet I still feel scared, like maybe I should have gone out on my own a bit before we got engaged. In a way, I've had it easier than most of my friends who are still out there looking for Mr. Right. I've never had to struggle."

These are very legitimate fears—if you are marrying young, you have a different kind of responsibility to your own growth and future development as a person than someone who is older and has struggled with these issues on her own before.

□ *Sex and the Single Girl*

Marriage may also occasion the emergence of fears relating to your sexuality identity and attractiveness to men in general. (Rest assured, your fiancé is probably experiencing the same kinds of fears). Not only will you and your partner have anxieties about becoming less sexually attractive to one another as a result of marriage—you may worry that familiarity and habit will spell the end of desire—but you may also be fearful about your sexual attractiveness as far as the rest of the world is concerned.

Now this may seem like a contradiction, because, on the eve of marriage, why would you be worried about being sexually attractive to other people? And yet it is precisely the same sense of self-worth, confidence, and pride that comes from being a sexually attractive woman (or man) in the world that makes you feel sexy to your mate at home. Put another way: It's easy to feel sexy for your partner when you know that the rest of the world finds you sexy. But doesn't marriage change all that? Won't marriage make people think of you as "a wife"—which is already a more desexualized term than "girlfriend" or "lover"? "I know that men have always found me attractive," says twenty-seven-year-old Phyllis, an aspiring actress with several commercials to her credit. "It has nothing to do with whether I'm attracted to them, but I just like knowing they feel that way. It's like money in the bank—it gives me a sense of security. I guess I'm afraid I'll have to give all that up when I get married, and I don't like thinking about it."

Couples fear that marriage will be the end of romance and passionate sexuality between them. And indeed, one of the most important challenges for the soon-to-be married couple is learning to maintain an ongoing erotic connection within the context of a long-term, complex, and multifaceted relationship. Paradoxically enough, it is often easier to have a powerful sexual response to someone you do not know well at all—this allows you to project your fantasies onto that person. But a fiancé—who will soon become a spouse, a mate, a partner for life—presents a vastly more complicated set of emotional factors with which each partner must learn to contend. In a way, you have to work at keeping the

*romance alive in the midst of the often hectic domestic
schedule you will both soon share."*

◆

□ *Keep the Home Fires Burning*

Consider these ways to keep the sexy feelings from being
submerged by fear:

◆ Don't put off romance and pleasure in your relationship for the weekends or vacations. Too many couples
have gotten in the habit of putting their romantic and
sexual lives on hold five days a week. This leads to a sense
of deprivation and a terrific pressure on the weekend.
Hard as it may be for you to unwind from your busy
careers, it really is essential for the ongoing vitality of the
relationship that you do so.

◆ Don't be afraid of enacting erotic fantasies with your
fiancé. It's all too easy to de-eroticize your partner in the
context of the humdrum daily existence—taking out the
garbage, raking the leaves, applying for a mortgage, or
paying the bills are necessary domestic responsibilities,
but hardly sexy. Fight back against the familiarity of your
shared life: Be playful, be inventive, and encourage each
other to explore hidden desires. Although you may think
you know the sexual appetites of your beloved, there is
always room for discovery and experimentation.

◆ Do make sex, and sexuality, a part of your vocabulary.
As surprising as this may sound, many couples find that

verbal references to lovemaking that has taken place or lovemaking that is anticipated is an extremely charged part of their erotic connection. Sexy talk—references to body parts and to pleasurable sexual activities—can be a wonderful aphrodisiac. Don't underestimate the power of the word!

□ *The Body Beautiful*

Closely allied to fears concerning sexuality is the one about physical fitness in general. Often women (and men, too) remain weight-and-fitness conscious in the hope of attracting and securing a mate. Having successfully accomplished this, it is easy to fear that you will become somewhat more lax about your physical appearance. "When I went to Italy, I was shocked to see how so many beautiful young girls seemed to age thirty years once they became married women! It was as if they had given up on themselves after marriage," said Jessica, who went to Europe on her honeymoon. "Maybe they felt that they didn't need to care so much any more, but I certainly don't want that to happen to me. When Hank took one look at those women, he turned to me and said, 'I just want you to know I consider *that* grounds for divorce!' "

This fear is the physical counterpart to the emotional fear of losing your individuality after marriage: you may worry that you will lose the competitive edge that has kept you at your physical peak. You may also have a similar fear that your partner will succumb to this laxity as well, and the slim, trim bodybuilder you fell in love with will soon become flabby and unappealing.

☐ *A Modern-Day Juggling Act:*
  Career, Marriage, and Kids

Do not underestimate the effect that the women's movement has had, and continues to have, on your life, especially right now. Thanks to the social changes brought about in the last three decades, the expectations for you as a wife have changed dramatically. Whereas once it was assumed that marriage would effectively put the lid on any major career ambitions—your energy instead would have been directed toward home, children, and the career of your husband—that is no longer the case today. On the contrary, today's wife is envisioned as a kind of Superwoman: She'll have a brilliant career, while remaining a sexy and supportive wife, a superlative homemaker, and finally, a loving mother.

That is indeed a tall order, and may well inspire fear even in the most confident of brides-to-be. "My mother had her hands full with the three of us," says twenty-eight-year-old Elissa, who was born and raised in Los Angeles. "We were her full-time job. But Ken and I both have pretty demanding jobs—I am a free-lance screen writer, and Ken owns and manages his own restaurant—and I know that when we get married, we'll both have to pitch in to get the housework and the cooking done. I feel that even now, I have more different kinds of responsibilities to handle than my mother did. I worry about how we'll manage when we decide to have kids."

□ *"What's in a Name?"*

Not the least important of the questions that the women's movement has raised is whether a woman is going to take her husband's name as her own.

Once upon a time, all women who got married took their husband's names. Just as their mothers and grandmothers before them. But times have indeed changed, and the number of women who opt to keep their own names is growing.

Many women, especially those with any kind of professional stature, are fearful about giving up the name—and with it the identity—that has always been theirs. "I've worked too hard to get where I am," says thirty-three-year-old Gayle, who teaches history at a midwestern university. "If someone saw my married name on an academic article, they would not know it was the same person: that would bother me a lot. I can't help but want all the people I've ever known to recognize me." Gayle's story is similar to that of many professional women—movie and TV writers, academics, journalists— who have used one name under which to publish and hesitate about assuming a new one.

Based on the premise that a name change represents a loss of self, the decision to keep one's own name has gone from being an oddity to a frequently used option. "I like my name," says French-born Sabine Marceux, "especially living in the United States. It keeps me in touch with my cultural heritage, which is very important to me. I don't want to give it up, even for the man I love."

Yet even given the changing social climate, many women still prefer to take the name of the man they are marrying. "It's the traditional thing to do," says one woman, "and deep down, I consider myself a very traditional person." And twenty-six-year-old Connie, whose parents divorced when she was seven, adds this; "I haven't been close to my father; he left when I was a little girl and I haven't seen him in years. Having his name doesn't mean much to me. On the contrary, now that I'm getting married, I want the name that symbolizes my new attachment and my new family. Some of my friends have criticized me for my decision, but that's what feels right, so that's what I'm going to do."

There is no right or wrong choice here; what is important is that you understand the emotional implications of your choice and discuss them with your fiancé before the wedding. If you find yourself burdened with other, larger fears now—such as the ones discussed above—delay making this decision until later.

What to Do

Addressing your fears won't ever be easy, but here are some ways to get a handle on your feelings:

◆ As you did with your anxieties, you and your fiancé should attempt to make a list of all the things that are making you fearful during this period. This may be difficult to do because it is often the nature of these fears to remain hidden. You might not be consciously aware of your fears about not living up to the kind of marriage your parents had or about your sexual attractiveness. Instead, you may be entirely focused on the details of the wedding to the exclusion of all else. For instance, Patrick was not aware that he was feeling especially fearful before his wedding to Trish. But when during the engagement party he joked that his biggest worry was that Trish's wedding gown would be cut too low, she felt hurt and offended. She later questioned him about it and he insisted that she was making too much of what had been an off-handed remark. But Trish persisted. "You never minded that I looked sexy before we were engaged," she pointed out. "In fact, you used to like it. Do you trust me less now than you did then?" Upon examination, however, it turned out to be an issue of fear, rather than of trust. Patrick was afraid that if Trish appeared too available to other men once they were married, his own masculinity would somehow be placed in question. He feared other men would interpret her sexy clothes as an indication that he failed to satisfy her. None of this was immediately apparent to either Patrick or Trish: It took a step-by-step dismantling of the external evidence—in this case, a remark made at a party—to reveal the fear hidden beneath the surface behavior. If you can remain sensitive to your partner's seemingly irrelevant fears (and your own), you will be better able to uncover the deeper feelings they are usually masking.

You may now have a better idea of the kinds of fears

that are apt to be brewing. Discuss these openly and honestly with your fiancé and encourage him to do the same. While you may not come up with any concrete suggestions instantly, simply by articulating your fears you have already moved toward neutralizing their potency.

♦ Don't feel compelled to make hard and fast decisions about married life; you are already under enough stress from simply trying to deal with all the emotions that are surfacing as you plan the wedding. Talking about having children, for example, is not only premature, but may also serve to enhance your fears during this time. Discourage family members and friends from making probing inquiries like "So when do you plan to start your family?" with a polite but firm, "We're taking it one step at a time, and we haven't gotten to that one yet."

♦ If possible, don't make any other major life changes during this time. Put off looking for a new job right now. Of course, you may not have complete control of your present job situation, particularly if you are asked to assume significant new responsibilities. "I had wanted this promotion so badly that when it came along—six weeks before the wedding, I jumped at the chance," says twenty-nine-year-old Louise, who for the last five years has worked in the human resources department of a mid-sized public relations firm. The step up took the form of advancement to director of the division—a position for which she felt fully qualified and was eager to assume. "All of a sudden I had to adjust to a whole new level at work—late meetings, managing a department of five people, complete accountability for my area—on top of trying to plan and prepare for the wedding. I was running around like a crazy person all the time; there was just so much on my shoulders, I felt like I couldn't cope. One morning I looked in the refrigerator and when I found I was out of milk, I burst into tears!" What Louise—and you, should you find yourself in this situation—needs to remember is the importance of being able to separate your fears. Don't use your new position as a vehicle to express your fears about the wedding and don't use the wedding as a way to express your fears about the new job. For example, if you find yourself crying about your job or becoming testy with coworkers, or on the other hand, complaining about your fiancé's wardrobe and vocabulary—things that don't ordinarily bother you in the least, it's time to slow down and sort things out. The odds are that a great deal of displacement is going on. Once it's clear which problems are specifically work related and which are about the wedding, it will be a relatively straightforwrd process to iron out the difficulties.

◆ Don't be alarmed if you (or your partner) seem to need the ego-boost of harmless flirting with members of the opposite sex. If you find that the flirtation becomes more persistent and flagrant, then you may be headed for trouble. But don't jump to conclusions until you have real reason to doubt your fiancé's fidelity or his feelings for you. This shouldn't be confused with a serious dissatisfaction with your partner (or a sexual interest in anyone else), but instead may be an unconscious antidote to the fears about sexual attractiveness after marriage. Understand, too, that sometimes the positive reactions of other people can work as an aphrodisiac for the two of you. Says one woman: "I know that my fiancé's best friend thinks I'm pretty sexy. There's absolutely nothing between us and I've never encouraged him, but I've noticed that after an evening the three of us have spent together, my fiancé is always wildly passionate when we get home!"

• If you are conscious of feeling apprehensive about your sexual desirability and attractiveness in general, use this time to give yourself some extra-special physical pampering. Indulge in a new haircut, facial, massage—whatever it takes to make you feel glamorous and sexy. And while it isn't good to add the pressures of a rigorous physical regime if you are not accustomed to it, you may want to consider joining a gym or health club *after* the wedding (make it a dual membership to encourage him to stay fit as well!) as a private pledge to maintaining your own sense of pride in your body and the way it looks.

• If you have been able to identify your fears as either stemming from a concern about a surrender of your single life or conversely giving up the chance for the kind of single life you never had, keep this in mind: Marriage doesn't have to mean the ultimate subordination of who you are to another person. If you were accustomed to being independent and self-reliant before the engagement, there is no reason you cannot assume some of the same prerogatives within marriage. And even if you are young and haven't really tried your wings, you can still make a conscious effort to keep growing and developing—maintaining separate friendships, making career strides, continuing your education—even after you are married. In both cases, the attention paid to yourself will ultimately pay off in your marriage.

7.

FRUSTRATION:

Is It Really This Hard to Get Married?

◆

At this point, you and your fiancé are probably deep in the throes of planning your wedding. For many couples, making the nitty-gritty decisions is the most trying part of the whole process, and one that seems to elicit the strongest emotional reactions.

You're already familiar with a number of the myriad emotions of the hectic prenuptial period: elation and anxiety, jealousy and fear. In this chapter, you will come to understand how all these feelings together add up to create an emotional powder keg. The fuses that often set it off are the seemingly inconsequential details of the wedding day itself.

□ *Seeming Trifles*

As you have probably already discovered the hard way, the little details involved in planning your wedding may cause you and your fiancé the greatest psychological turmoil. Everyone connected to this event—and you must of course include yourselves at the top of this list—has an opinion and is eager, sometimes to the point of insistence, upon sharing it.

First and foremost, you must understand that *none* of the decisions you make will be neutral. From the largest issues to the smallest, every decision has a tremendous emotional significance.

Some of the wedding decisions you are now called upon to make are more overtly emotional ones, but many of them are disguised as practical ones (Where do we get married? Who marries us? What kind of wedding reception do we want?, and the like), so you can easily be thrown off track. And yet, the intensity of feelings these issues elicit—how many fights have you had already over the seating arrangements or the wording of the ceremony?—should clue you in to the fact that *all* these decisions have a powerful psychological meaning. "Is it really possible to get so agitated over the color of the napkins?" you may ask yourself more than once as you move through the busy weeks ahead. The answer is yes, if you accept the fact that the napkins, and every other picayune detail about your wedding, is really just a vessel through which all your deepest feelings are expressed.

□ *Rules of the Game*

Before beginning to discuss the actual pitfalls of planning your wedding, it is important to take note of how the planning of weddings has undergone a radical transformation in recent years. As a bride-to-be of the 1990s, you are likely to be: older than brides of a previous generation; living in a different city from your family; and accustomed to making your own choices. You and your fiancé may also be footing the bill for the wedding yourselves, as has been discussed in chapter 3. In addition to all that, you are probably holding down a full-time job during the entire engagement period. The option of having six months in which you do nothing but plan a wedding is, alas, a luxury most women nowadays probably won't get to enjoy.

Heidi, a thirty-three-year-old fund-raiser for a large philanthropic organization based in New York City, is a good example. "It just worked out that I was planning the wedding during one of our key fund-raising campaigns, which meant that I was running around shopping for a dress and shoes in between hopping on and off planes. I think I took four trips in six weeks! And since my family lives out in Seattle, they really couldn't be of much help." While Heidi could have elected to use her vacation time to plan the wedding, it would have meant postponing her honeymoon indefinitely. "At the time, Dennis and I decided that we really wanted a nice, long honeymoon, but in retrospect, I might have done it differently. It was pretty hellish trying to arrange the wedding in the midst of so much pressure at work; it was like holding down two full-time jobs."

Even if your schedule isn't quite as hectic as Heidi's, it can still be difficult to hold down a nine-to-five job when you're trying to plan your wedding, as twenty-seven-year-old Carmen who works long hours as an assistant buyer in a Chicago department store, found out. "At work, I'm all over the place—out on the floor, in the stockroom, checking on the arrival of new shipments. I rarely have a chance to sit quietly at my desk, and so it was hard placing calls to the caterer, the florist, and all the rest of the people I needed to contact. And by the time I got through with work at seven or eight, it was too late already. So that left me just one free day each week— Saturday—to get everything done. Did I feel crazed? You bet!"

As a result of this kind of stress, you may be feeling overwhelmed, angry, or just plain frustrated. How can you plan a wedding when you still have to go to work and do a good job every day? Here are some ideas about how to cope:

◆ If you haven't already done so, tell your boss and/or coworkers that you are in the midst of planning your wedding. Don't use this as an excuse for work that is poorly done; rather, offer it as an explanation in the hopes of gaining a little leeway. For instance, perhaps you can postpone a certain business trip until after the wedding. Or eat lunch at your desk so you can leave early to get a head start on running your errands. In any case, it will look better to state your situation clearly up front than to have your boss or colleagues wondering about why you seem distracted or preoccupied.

♦ Although Heidi wanted to save her vacation time for a long, leisurely honeymon, you may consider taking a few days—or even half-days—away from the job if you're feeling especially harassed. Otherwise, you could find yourself too burned-out from the wedding preparations to properly enjoy the honeymoon. It's all too easy to keep saying, "We'll relax on the honeymoon" as a way of dealing with the hectic prewedding period, but if you let yourselves become too exhausted now, you will enjoy neither the wedding nor the honeymoon that follows it.

♦ Consider getting outside help for some of your prewedding chores. Do remember, however, that asking for help opens you up to potentially unwelcome interference from well meaning family and friends; since this is usually a greater danger with family than friends, you may want to turn to friends first. Yet despite the risk, it can be worth dealing with this emotional situation if it buys you a much needed pair of extra hands. Keep the chores specific and concrete. Unless you truly do not have a strong preference, don't ask your sister, or mother, to select the flowers for the centerpieces; that would be giving her too much power over your wedding. Instead, ask one of them if she can find out what flowers will be in season and what they will cost.

♦ Without compromising on the things you feel are essential, look over your "to-do" list to see where you might be able to simplify. Is it really necessary to drive all the way from New York to Pennsylvania to borrow your great aunt's heirloom silver cake server? Can you accept ordering the cake from a local bakery, rather than one that is over eighty miles away and is unable to deliver? If you can eliminate some of the most time-consuming and needlessly worrisome details from the planning, the whole process is apt to move more smoothly.

□ *Division of Labor*

Since traditionally the wedding was made by the family of the bride, much of today's wedding planning now falls to the bride herself, as the natural exponent of her family. But for the reasons discussed above, this is likely to create a frustrating situation in which you feel overwhelmed by the responsibility for the entire event.

Even before you think of asking friends and family to help, you will naturally turn to the person closest to you: your fiancé. And while, ideally, this should represent a perfect option—after all, who better than the prospective groom, your chosen partner, to share the planning of the wedding with?—often, reality doesn't coincide with this prettily painted picture.

The simple fact is that many of the essential details—food, flowers, dress, and the like—are still, even in this so-called liberated age, considered to be the province of women. And although your fiancé might care about the wedding in theory, when it comes down to it, he may claim utter indifference to many of the finer points. "Does she really expect me to get excited over the table settings and the lettering on the invitations?" says one groom-to-be. "Please, give me a break!"

On the other hand, you may find that if you go ahead and make decisions by yourself, your fiancé can feel angry and usurped, even though he may have cheerfully declined to make his feelings and opinions known. Says twenty-five-year-old Irene of her fiancé: "When I asked Barry his opinion about the menu at the reception or the color of the candles at the tables, he got annoyed that I was pestering him with 'all the trivia.' So after a while, I stopped asking and started making some choices on my own. But then he got upset that I had made decisions without consulting him! 'I thought we were supposed to be a team,' he told me. No matter what I did, it seemed like it was a no-win situation."

Irene's situation is hardly unusual. Many brides find that what poses as a shared responsibility is often just a pretense for both partners taking the credit while one does the lion's share of the work.

Overcoming this problem depends in large part on simply recognizing it and pointing it out to your partner. You need to remind him—gently—that if he wants a part in what's going on, he needs to make himself available for consultation, discussion, and expressing his preferences. If there are some things that really don't interest him—like the flowers you're going to be carrying—focus on the things that *do:* the guest list or the kind of ceremony you are planning.

If he still fails to show interest, you may have to resign yourself to doing most of the work yourself. But then he must understand that he has forfeited the option to complain if things are not to his liking. You have to stress that if he wants his wishes to be considered and respected, he has to assume the responsibility for their expression.

Though less common, it is possible that you will find yourself in the opposite situation: You may have a fiancé who has such definite opinions on all aspects of the wedding that his taste threatens to dominate your own. Twenty-three-year-old Toni found that her thirty-year-old fiancé, Matt, had something definitive to say about everything they discussed. "Matt is a landscape gardener and is very proud of his taste," says Toni, "so at first I really welcomed his input. But when he started in on the dress that I would be wearing, it really got to be too much!"

An overly involved fiancé is as problematic—or even more so—as the one who claims he just doesn't care. In such a situation, it is important that you assert your own preferences about the wedding and demand to be given an equal voice in arranging it. Not only is the wedding itself a joint venture, the details of which should be mutually pleasing to both of you, but learning to compromise and resolve the differences now will be good preparation for the marriage that lies ahead.

□ *Quantity: How Many People Do We Invite?*

The size of your wedding would seem to be a purely practical issue of logistics. "What can we afford?" and "Where can we find an appropriate space?" are the two operative questions here. But there are nevertheless emotional ramifications engendered by your decision, which might not be at all apparent. Here, for instance, are three different options regarding the size of the wedding and some of the emotional issues that they raise.

1. *The Big Wedding*

Having a big wedding—anything larger than fifty people—will give you the sense of being embraced by the world of people whom you care about and love. Lydia and Douglas went all out and had a wedding at which there were more than two hundred people present. "It was fabulous!" recalls Lydia. "And our guests seemed to be having as good a time as we were." And Douglas adds, "It gave us the chance to see people we hadn't seen in ages and to really let loose and celebrate. It was the best party I've ever been to." Both Lydia and Douglas described themselves as outgoing, gregarious types; they enjoyed being the center of attention, and big, noisy parties gave them both a thrill. For this pair, the decision to have a large wedding was the perfect choice emotionally as well as practically.

But you also have to understand that the bigger the wedding, the less opportunity you will have to share your experience individually with each of the guests. You may well feel like a performer at your own wedding, charged with the responsibility of meeting and greeting an endless sea of faces while the real event slips imperceptibly by. This was the experience of Jamie and Neil, whose parents together chipped in for a gala wedding to which almost three hundred guests were invited. "It was a mistake," says soft-spoken Jamie. "There were just too many people to deal with. I felt that by the time I had gotten around to saying hello to everyone, the wedding was over." And Neil, who shares Jamie's sense of personal reserve, adds, "By the end of the day, I felt like the smile on my face was going to fall on the floor and break. Instead of the wedding day being a joy, it turned into a kind of marathon—I kept looking at my watch and thinking, 'When will they all just leave so we can relax and be alone?'" Clearly, neither Neil nor Jamie had the kind of personality that was suited to an event of these proportions; for them, a smaller wedding would have been the wiser emotional choice.

2. *The Small Wedding*

A wedding of fewer than fifty people tends to feel more intimate, cozy, and manageable. You can expect to feel that a wedding of this size is well within your emotional control. This was certainly the case for Felicia and Scott, who were married on a warm May afternoon in the presence of twenty-five close relatives and friends. "It was just perfect," says Felicia. "We couldn't have had a better time. Everyone we really loved was there, and the whole day was just so comfortable and relaxed. My sister had her two daughters with her and Scott's brother brought his nephew and niece; after the ceremony, all the kids had fun running around together on the lawn. Somehow, seeing them playing together like that seemed to be such a good omen for *our* marriage."

But small weddings are not without their emotional drawbacks. Since life doesn't offer that many opportunities to have a big celebration, you just may feel that you've been cheated out of one if you opt for a small wedding. And you may also experience feelings of guilt about people whom you weren't able to invite.

3. *The Two-for-One Wedding*

Consider this alternative as a chance to have your cake and eat it, too. You can opt for a small ceremony at which only family members and close friends are present and then throw a big party later on to celebrate your newly wedded state. Certainly, this choice will alleviate the guilt involved with the small wedding and the sense of alienation that can come with a large one. And for some couples, like Sean and Christina, this was the perfect emotional option. The couple got married in a small ceremony in Christina's hometown in Georgia. "Only our immediate families were there," remembers Christina, "and I had such a sense of the importance of what we were doing. It felt very intimate and even holy." Later on, when she and Sean returned to Washington, D.C., where they lived, they had a big party for all their friends and other relatives. "The party was a different kind of event," says Christina. "Because we had already gotten married two weeks before, we weren't a bit nervous. Yet we were able to enjoy the experience all over again; in a way, it was like getting married twice."

But some couples—Chip and Holly are a good example—find that the responsibility of planning two separate events makes them feel even more overwhelmed and frustrated. Chip's family was from Maine and Holly's from Missouri; the couple had been living first in New York, but six months prior to the wedding, they moved to San Francisco. "We were literally all over the map," says Holly. "First we had to find a convenient place to have the wedding, since my parents are pretty old and weren't up to much traveling. So we got married in Kansas City, because it was nearby to where my folks live. Then, when we planned the party, it was an even bigger problem, because most of our friends were in New York. Could we really ask all those people to fly out, especially when the ceremony had already taken place? Where were we going to put them up? It didn't seem feasible, so we had to fly back from San Franciso to the East Coast after the wedding. There were too many things to orchestrate; if we could do it over, I would consolidate the plans a little better."

□ Quality: Whom Will We Invite?

Believe it or not, sitting down to prepare the guest list is one of the most hazardous points on the road to marriage. More arguments ensue and more tempers flare—between you and your fiancé, your parents, his parents, other relatives, and friends—than at any other point along the way.

Before you write the first name or attach a single stamp to an invitation, take note of what has been the central theme of the entire engagement period: You and your fiancé are embarking upon this wedding first and foremost for yourselves. Others are invited to share, enjoy, participate, and revel—never to take over or dominate. It is a question of priorities here, and yours and your fiancé's have to come first.

Although it may be hard for you to put your foot down about the guests, it is essential that you *do,* and that you do it *early.* If you can afford to invite everyone on your, your fiancé's, and both your parents' lists, you should do exactly that, provided that what you really want is a big wedding. But since most people are working with limited funds, this is not a realistic alternative. Instead, you will have to develop a cut-off point and stick to it. You can expect this to lead to some difficulties with family and friends. But far worse is the scenario in which you are surrounded by people who mean little to you personally—business associates of your father's, relatives you last saw twenty years ago, or have never even met—and are deprived of the presence of those who really do mean a lot. Here are a few thoughts on how to structure a guest list for maximum emotional satisfaction and minimal stress:

◆ *Family.* While chapter 3 addressed the issue of how to cope with divorced parents and children from previous marriages during this period, there is still the question of the rest of your respective families. Not only siblings, but grandparents, aunts, uncles, and cousins are all going to be the subject of much conversation right now.

First, as discussed earlier, the act of marriage establishes a new family unit: You and your beloved are joining together to form a separate entity within the larger family circle. You and your fiancé can use the wedding as an opportunity to make a statement about your new roles within the family. The choice of guests is a symbolic statement about who you are within the family and how you want to be regarded. This is a moment for setting precedents and shaping the future; you can use it to declare your alliances and feelings of intimacy with various family members. If you truly don't feel close to a particular group of cousins, you should not feel obligated—or allow yourself to be pressured—to invite them to your wedding, no matter what your family says.

Unconsciously, your parents (and those of your fiancé) perceive the meaning of the new bond that is being made—that is precisely why they may try to exert so much control over which family members are invited to the wedding. Knowing this may help you understand why the subject of the guest list can become so volatile.

Naturally, if you are from extremely close families, you will want to invite everyone. But rare is the family nowadays that remains both intimate and within a geographical proximity. Just because you were once close, are you obligated to invite your third cousin, last seen when you both had braces and pigtails? There are two basic options here—reunion or exclusion—and each has its emotional ramifications.

The emotional pleasures of a family reunion are obvious: You get a chance to see people whom you haven't laid eyes on in ages, and in the joy-filled context of your wedding. Many, many couples say that this kind of reunion was one of the happiest aspects of the wedding.

Yet the negative emotions that stem from gathering together far-flung family members are also a consideration, although these may be less immediately apparent. Each time you see a family member whom you haven't seen in years, there is an emotional toll to be paid. You may find yourself plunged back into a past that you just may not want to be reliving on your wedding day. It is also possible that you will be unfairly judged by some relative—to a greater or lesser degree—on the basis of the man you have chosen to marry. "He's not very good-looking"; "He certainly doesn't make much money"; and "She could have done better" are easily the kinds of things your relatives are capable of thinking and somehow manage to convey. And even if your relatives are not thinking these things, it is almost inevitable that you will feel that they are. The closer you are to the relative, the less probable it is that you will be harshly judged as a result of whom you've chosen; the more distant the connection, the more likely you are to be subject to this kind of clinical scrutiny. This in not an especially comforting or happy thought, and so it is worthwhile deciding early on just how much of this kind of judgmental atmosphere you are willing to put up with—or forgo—on your wedding day.

Finally, don't be fooled by one of the most common—and easily the most wrong-headed—clichés about weddings ever to be put forth: "It will break my mother's heart if I don't invite Great Uncle Clarence." Contrary to your worst expectations, it won't! This may seem like heresy, but the fact is this: The absence of your Uncle Clarence or Cousin Harriet will NOT permanently damage your mother's heart. Although they may carry on a bit, mothers and fathers are remarkably resilient and incredibly forgiving when the wedding day rolls around.

◆ *Friends.* As you are learning from dealing with your extended families, you have to establish a cut-off point somewhere when you are chosing the friends you want to invite. You simply can't invite every single member of your Girl Scout troop or all of your fiancé's tennis cronies, nor would you want to. Keep in mind that the issue of feeling unfairly judged by your guests applies equally well to friends as it does to family. And, as with your family, while this can be an ideal opportunity to renew your bond with your freshman roommate or high school pals, it may entail the same kinds of emotional pressures and hazards.

◆ *Colleagues and Business Associates.* By inviting the people with whom you work, you will radically shift the tone of your wedding. From being a basically intimate and personal event, it will now be one that incorporates the elements of professional alliance, power, and networking. Such a shift is not necessarily a bad one, but you need to be fully aware of it before you do it. For some couples, this does not represent a significant emotional issue, because their coworkers are also their closest friends. Twenty-nine-year-old Jill is an architect with a small firm in Rhode Island. Her boss is one of her former teachers; the two other architects in the firm have become, in the three years they have worked together, dear friends. "I can't imagine not having the whole gang

at my wedding," she says. "They've become like family."
Clearly, Jill's choice was an easy one emotionally: The
professional and the personal aspects of her life were
happily allied.

But what happens when you work for a larger, less
closely knit company? Joanna, thirty-one, is employed in
the policy-writing division of a large Milwaukee insurance
agency. "There are people from other areas that I've never
even met," she says in describing the firm. "And we're
all pretty formal here—it's Miss and Mister for everyone;
no first names. I'd like to invite the two people I share
an office with, but I'm worried that some other people
in my department will find out and feel offended that I
didn't ask *them*. I'm really not sure what to do." Joanna
needs to realize that there is nothing wrong with inviting
only some and not all—of the people she works with.
In so doing, she is making an honest declaration about
the people to whom she feels personally close, but she
is in no way saying she can't work effectively—or even
in time become friends—with all the people in her division.

It is also possible for Joanna—or you—to decide
that she doesn't want to mix her professional and her
personal life at all. If you really don't enjoy the company
of your coworkers, or if your present work has unpleasant
associations (You're unhappy with the nature of your re-
sponsibilites, are bored, overwhelmed, or don't get along
with your superiors), then the best choice might be to
maintain the separation between the personal and the
professional. For workaholics, this could even be a

healthy beginning of a stronger home life after the wedding day has come and gone.

◆ *Escorts.* Traditionally, the guests invited to your wedding would be accompanied by a spouse, or, if unmarried, by a member of the opposite sex. But what do you do in an age when so many people are allied in what can be best described as nontraditional relationships? Twenty-seven-year-old Mary has two brothers—one older and one younger—who were both planning to attend her wedding. Since her older brother is married already, the issue of his escort was easily solved. But Mary's younger brother is gay, and although his immediate family was aware of this fact, many of the aunts, uncles, and cousins who were being invited (from Mary's family and that of her fiancé) were not. Mary's mother wanted her brother to bring a woman—any woman—as his escort, just to keep the family from finding out. But Mary, who is close to that brother, wanted to invite her brother's male lover as his escort, to the dismay of both families. "I know what they expected to have happen," Mary says, "Rick's being gay is supposed to be this big secret. But I find that offensive and demeaning; I just won't do that to my brother." Over the objections of the two families, Rick and his lover attended—and thoroughly enjoyed—Mary's wedding. But Mary had to be willing to endure the disapproval of her family and to stick to her guns when they tried to persuade her to change her mind.

You may be faced with other nontraditional relationships involving your guests, such as couples who live together but are not married, though few will be as volatile a subject as a gay couple. Escorts for those not permanently attached also present potential emotional problems. Do you only invite the boyfriend or girlfriend of your chums if they are formerly engaged, but not if they are simply living together? Or if they have been a couple for six months but not for six weeks? There is no right or wrong in this situation: If you prefer your guests to bring only a spouse or fiancé, you are free to impose that as a rule. But be prepared for tempers to flare and feelings to be wounded when someone is excluded. You may find that you have to defend or explain your decision not once but several times during the prewedding period.

☐ *Musical Chairs*

Next to selecting the guests to be invited, deciding who will sit where seems to be high up on the list of things to fight about. You may wonder why this is so; after all, it's only for one afternoon or evening, so why is everyone getting so upset about it?

First of all, understand that the issue of seating arrangements at the wedding touches upon some very basic psychological issues of power and allegiance within the larger family unit. Because the seating plan establishes—if only for the brief duration of the wedding—an emotional hierarchy everyone is apt to be very touchy about it. "Who is where" seems to raise feelings about who is the most loved and most valued member of the family. Even though you and your fiancé may not feel this way, you can be sure that everyone else involved in the wedding *will*. The sooner you understand that this is not a minor issue emotionally—but that in fact a great deal is at stake—the easier it will be for you to cope.

Here are four practical options about how to handle the seating arrangements at the reception and the emotional implications that each of these choices entail:

1. *The Sit-Down Meal with Place Cards*

This has become the standard seating arrangement, and for the reasons described above, is the one that creates the most emotional complications. "My parents were so insistent that my uncles and aunts be included at our table that when I suggested the group was getting too big—I have a number of brothers and sisters, and so does my fiancé—my mother actually hung up on me!" says twenty-eight-year-old Yvonne. "I couldn't believe she would act that way. The fact is, I'm really not that close to my uncles and aunts; instead, I wanted my friends from England—they were flying in just for the wedding and I don't get to see them that often—to sit with us." What Yvonne—and you—must remember is a point that has been made many times in this book. As you and your fiancé are planning the wedding primarily for yourselves, the seating arrangement, like any other decision, should first reflect your priorities.

Before you and your fiancé discuss the seating with your families, the two of you should carefully design a seating configuration that is meaningful to the two of you. Your wedding table should be comprised of the people who mean the most to the two of you, not to your parents, and can be a group made of both family and friends. Present your seating arrangement to your families as an essentially fixed plan. Make alterations if they seem reasonable and only if they don't infringe upon your feelings.

Finally, whatever the final arrangement is, you can help to mitigate the kind of hierarchy established by the seating plan by making it a point to change tables and circulate with all your guests after the meal is over.

2. *The Sit-Down Meal without Place Cards*

If you abandon the notion of place cards (this usually works best with a buffet meal), you have in effect done away with the rigidity of the seating plan. Instead, your guests are free to sit where they choose. While this takes the onus off you before the wedding, it can create a somewhat awkward situation for the guests, especially for those who don't know many people. As a result, you may find that you and your fiancé have a greater social obligation on the wedding day itself, mingling with the guests and making sure that they feel comfortable.

In addition, a meal without place cards can create an emotional free-for-all, with guests unsure or even competitive about where they sit. And although it may appear to be the more-relaxed alternative, it can easily turn into a disorderly affair, lacking in a sense of ceremony and decorum.

3. *Wedding à la Cocktail Party*

While considered the least formal of the four alternatives, this option has some distinct emotional advantages. A cocktail-style wedding completely does away with the difficulties of the seating arrangement, and the food you serve here can be as substantial and elaborate as at a sit-down meal. Instead, guests are able to mingle comfortably; even people who don't know others will find it more comfortable to talk to someone standing next to them than to make conversation with someone they don't know for an entire meal.

As a result of this relaxed atmosphere, you and your fiancé are apt to feel very relaxed yourselves. Says Sonia, who worried that the stand up reception she and her fiancé, James, planned wouldn't work out: "We did it because we got married at my mother's apartment and there simply wasn't enough space to seat the seventy-five people we had invited. But the success of the wedding day exceeded our wildest expectations! Everyone had a wonderful time meeting and talking to everyone else— there was such a warm, congenial feeling to the event. I was so happy to see all these people that I loved finally getting a chance to meet and talk to one another. What started out as an issue of practicality ended up as a truly wonderful experience."

Also be aware that a stand-up reception usually means that guests leave in stages. There will be those who depart right after the ceremony, those who stay through the cake cutting, and finally a small group—usually those nearest and dearest to the couple—who remain until the very end of the reception. This gradual exodus again contributes to the relaxed feeling of the event; guests are free to participate in as much of the day as they choose, without feeling awkward about leaving.

On the other hand, you may find that your wedding has turned into just another cocktail party, rather than being the momentous occasion that you certainly want it to be.

4. *The Cake-and-Champagne Wedding*

Although you may believe that dispensing with a full-course meal at your wedding is in defiance of tradition, this is actually not the case. The fact is that simply serving cake and champagne after the ceremony is a perfectly traditional—and emotionally viable—choice for a wedding reception. As with the cocktail-style wedding described above, a reception of this kind allows your guests to mingle and talk comfortably with one another. And because you have limited the refreshments, you may well be able to afford to invite many more people than if you opted for a full meal.

Often, a cake-and-champagne wedding is preceded by a more elaborate rehearsal dinner the evening before the wedding. And if you are inviting many guests from out of town, you can include them in this event as well so that they will have a more extended sense of the wedding day.

□ *Of Altars and Alternatives*

Obviously, if you and your fiancé are from the same religious backgrounds, and are both observant, you will have a relatively easy time deciding on what kind of service you want.

But even couples who are from the same religious background can face these problems easily if neither one is particularly religious. Judy and Saul are both from nonobservant Jewish families. With the exception of a Bar Mitzvah, which, he says, was "more like a big thirteenth-birthday party," Saul had little religious training and Judy had even less. "My family celebrated Christmas!" she says. "They just weren't very religious Jews." But now that Judy and Saul are planning to get married, the religious question has come up again. "We both feel a little strange about the idea of being married by a rabbi," says Judy, "but the idea of being married by a minister is even stranger." And Saul adds, "We could opt for a civil ceremony, but we're not sure that feels right, either. We don't want to do away with all sense of ritual and sanctification in our wedding. It's a real problem." Judy and Saul eventually decided—with some misgivings—to be married by a liberal woman rabbi at the home they had shared for the past two years.

But if you are not from identical religious backgrounds, as is increasingly the case in our pluralistic society, the question of the ceremony is bound to be emotionally more complex. The practical solutions to this problem—and their emotional ramifications—can be summed up as follows:

◆ *You choose a religious service based on the partner who has the stronger religious connection: one partner may well choose to convert in order to accommodate the religious feelings of the other.* The decision to opt for the stronger religious feeling of the two or convert to a new religion can be seen as a joyful gift of marital commitment from one partner to another. You (or your fiancé) will feel loved, special, and respected because you (or he) will understand the nature of the sacrifice that has been made. This is not to say that you (or he) will necessarily feel like a martyr, but simply to point out the magnitude of the commitment that has been made to the other. When Evan, who was a disaffected Protestant, proposed to strongly Catholic Celia, he agreed to convert to Catholicism and be married by a priest. "It was actually a joy to undergo the conversion," says Evan. "Religion had never meant much in my family, but it meant a lot to Celia. I was happy I could participate in something that was so important to her. It really made us feel even closer. But at the same time, I have to say that changing religions isn't easy, even when you're not devout. I'm glad I did, and so is Celia, but it's nothing that you do lightly, no matter what you think in advance." And Celia adds, "I was deeply touched that Evan was willing to do that for me. I felt so loved. I had always hoped I would meet and fall in love with a Catholic, but now I'm glad it didn't turn out that way because I would never have felt cherished in the way I do now."

But this is no minor decision to make. If you are the one who decides to convert, not only will you have embarked upon a religion that is other than that of your upbringing—learning to accept both the dogma and customs of that faith—but you will have also performed a kind of radical psychic surgery on your own past. Even if you have drifted from the fold, you may only realize how important and formative your religious background has been when you have forfeited it in exchange for a new one.

This is precisely the kind of issue that may not seem problematic in the short run but may well turn into an emotional wedge over time. The partner who has given up his or her religion may come to resent the sense of strangeness and alienation that is attendant upon such a conversion. This is not meant to discourage you or your fiancé from such a decision, only to point out its emotional gravity.

If you are seriously considering conversion or even a service in a faith that is different from the one you were raised in, don't be hasty; spend a lot of time thinking and talking about it with your fiancé, family, and friends. It is also worthwhile to see a religious leader from the faith you are thinking of entering, to raise any questions or discuss any doubts you might have.

When Susan and Drew first became engaged, they planned to be married at his family's church in Boston.

Susan, who was Jewish, did not want to go through the formal ritual of conversion, but she nevertheless made an appointment to see Drew's minister in advance of the wedding. "It was when I was sitting there, face to face with the minister, that I realized I couldn't do it," says Susan. "I didn't have especially strong feelings about being Jewish, but I found out I had very strong feelings about not being Christian."

♦ *Two religious leaders perform the ceremony.* Opting for two leaders at the ceremony will create a sense of parity for both partners and their different pasts. Such a choice will make you feel equally proud of and comfortable with your various religious heritages. When Susan realized she was uncomfortable with the idea of an exclusively Christian service, she and Drew found a rabbi and minister who were willing to perform a joint ceremony at the home of Drew's parents. "For us, it was the perfect solution," says Susan, "and it even made our families happy—my folks were having real trouble with the idea of a church wedding—though that wasn't the reason we chose it."

♦ *You opt to have a civil ceremony.* A civil wedding—usually performed by a judge in his chambers (although some will make "house calls")—is the obvious and easiest answer for couples of differing religious backgrounds or without strong religious sentiment. While you may imagine that a civil ceremony will be cold and impersonal, many couples who have had one disagree: "Before we got married, Dave and I met with the judge," says Donna.

"He gave us a copy of the service he was going to use and said that if we had any changes to make, he'd be happy to accommodate us. He was willing to come to my parents' house—that's where we got married—and when he put on his robes, I really felt thrilled. It all seemed so solemn, and so real. He had a beautiful speaking voice—everyone said so later—and after the ceremony, he stayed for a glass of champagne and met both of our parents. It was a beautiful service."

☐ *Spirit of the Place*

Where you and your fiancé decide to get married is just as important as how. Once again, the place you select is bound to have some important emotional reasonance, so you should consider the following choices, and what they mean, before you decide.

◆ *Regal Rentals.* If you and the groom-to-be decide that you will rent a place in which to have your wedding, chances are neither of you will have any significant emotional ties to that place. This can be a real plus: Since you are embarking on a new life together and making a fresh start as a married couple, the lack of associations can be liberating, like a breath of emotional fresh air. You may find that renting a place—a hotel, hall, country club, community center, or private residence—is a symbol that points you both toward the future. Ted and Priscilla rented a large pleasure boat for their wedding, and were married at sea, under a sky filled with glittering stars. "It was heavenly!" sighs Priscilla. "The most romantic thing you could possibly imagine. Neither Ted nor I had ever done anything like that before—it was a new place and a new experience at the same time—and we really felt like we were sailing off into some magical future together."

But there is a downside to rented space as well: Renting a place to which you have no emotional ties may make you—and your guests—feel estranged and alienated from the events of the day. Peter and Doris, both longtime residents of New York City, rented an attractive Upper East Side town house for their wedding. "It was a lovely place," recalls Doris. "Everything was as elegant as could be—marble fireplaces, oak wainscotting, parquet floors in all the rooms." So what was the problem? "There was no meaning attached to anything," she says. "I felt like I was getting married on a stage set. During the reception, I found myself opening a door to what I thought was the bathroom. It turned out to be a broom closet, filled with buckets and mops and things. I thought to myself, 'What am I doing in this strange place? I don't belong here.'" Both Peter and Doris agreed that could they do it over again, they would try to find a place that had some emotional meaning for them.

♦ *Be It Ever so Humble* . . . Getting married at home—yours, your fiancé's, the one you already share, that of either of your parents or a close relative or friend—can be a wonderful, warm, and reassuring experience. On this most meaningful day, you will find yourselves in a place that is already endowed with many memories and strong emotional attachments. Home—with all its myriad associations of familiarity and intimacy—can be the literal embodiment of your most positive feelings about the wedding. That was the case for Bruce and Nina, who got married at the Virginia home of Bruce's parents. "It was a wonderful day," says Nina. "We both felt very relaxed and comfortable. Bruce's parents have a big, friendly house with lots of overstuffed chairs and sofas. We had the meal out on the lawn, and then when it started to get dark, everyone could come back in and get cozy. When the last guest left, Bruce and I curled up on the couch in the den and—with our wedding clothes still on—we actually fell asleep."

But the fact that you have feelings about the place can also make it more emotionally fraught and complex. And if you opt for a home wedding at any home other than your very own, your hosts—parents, friends, relatives—may use this as an opportunity to assume greater control of the planning. This can be a boon, because it will take the full burden of organizing the wedding off your shoulders. But as has been said many times, there is always a trade-off involved. If you want complete autonomy in planning the wedding, you must be ready to assume full responsibility for it as well; asking for help usually means surrendering a measure of your control.

There are other pitfalls to the home wedding, as Eddie and Lora discovered when they got married at the home of Lora's best friend, Sloane. "At first I was so happy when she offered her place for the wedding," says Lora. "She and her husband have this great old Victorian house in Saratoga Springs. It had plenty of room and a big backyard. What could have been more perfect?" Then what went wrong? "Eddie felt that Sloane—whom he was never crazy for—was running the whole show. He thought she didn't like his friends, and he just didn't feel right being in her house. I thought it would work out because the place itself was so special, but I guess that no place can overcome the people who own it. It didn't ruin our wedding, but I can see now that Eddie and I should have tried to find some place more neutral."

☐ *You Are What You Wear*

Whether you realize it or not, the image of a dazzling white wedding gown, train, and veil is one that still possesses a powerful emotional charge, even for the most liberated of women and often for their grooms as well. As we've seen in scores of Hollywood films, donning that white dress is considered the culmination of a woman's romantic life.

While it is true that this myth has undergone some revisionist thinking in recent years, and although you personally may have ceased to be swayed by it, you must nevertheless realize that whatever you decide to wear on your wedding day is going to be another emotional issue.

Traditionally, of course, brides wear white, a color that symbolizes spiritual purity, or even more literally, physical virginity. Because of this elaborate symbolic history, you may not feel comfortable wearing white, especially if you have had a sexual relationship with your fiancé or, as may well be the case, with other men in the past. Says thirty-three-year-old Jackie, who works as a technician at a large television network, "As a feminist, the idea of wearing white really rubbed me the wrong way. I very much move in a male world—women aren't usually expected to be technically competent in the way my job demands me to be—and I'm used to considering myself on equal terms with them. Wearing white is a throwback to some preliberation age, and I just won't do it."

For thirty-one-year-old Leslie, a second-time bride, wearing white has associations with her first wedding. "I bought the whole package last time: heirloom dress covered in pearls, sweeping train, veil, bouquet of white roses. A lot of good it did me when he left me for one of his coworkers at the office! I have very different feelings and expectations about this marriage, and I want that to be clear in what I choose to wear. So this time I'm wearing a bright red dress. Red is such a vibrant, exciting, 'I love life' sort of color, and that's just how I'm feeling right now. I've been keeping it a surprise from my family, because I know they'll disapprove. By the time they see me in it, it will be too late for them to say anything."

On the other hand, you should not let the symbolism of the color deter you from wearing it. You can allow yourself to enjoy the traditional aspect of wearing white even if you deny its literal meaning to your life. Twenty-nine-year-old Edith says this, "Casey and I lived together for over a year before we got engaged, and we made no secret of it. And before I knew Casey, I was in love with, and briefly lived with, someone else. Clearly, I'm not a sexual innocent anymore, and everyone at the wedding will know that. But I do consider myself a very traditional person—the ritual and ceremony of getting married are very important to me—and Casey and I are going to have a church wedding. Part of that means wearing white. I've never been married before, and I've never had the opportunity to wear a dress like that and I'm not going to miss it. I know some people would disagree—even my mother suggested that I consider wearing cream or another pastel, but I was firm. I'm going to be a bride and I want a white dress; it's just that simple."

Even beyond the color of your dress, there are other symbolic meanings the dress has come to assume. The wedding dress has traditionally been at the center of the bride's planning, preparation, and excitement about the wedding. Look in any bookstore or magazine shop, and you'll see entire publications devoted to finding, fitting, and buying the perfect wedding dress.

While it certainly is lovely to contemplate getting the right wedding dress, there is a subtle, unspoken message here: The perfect wedding dress is the embodiment and the assurance of the perfect wedding day. The media—television, movies, bridal and fashion magazines—contribute to the notion that if you buy the most beautiful dress in the world, you are guaranteed an equally beautiful wedding day, and even, by unconscious extension, married life.

So it is all the more important, then, to understand

that precisely *because* the "dress of your dreams" embodies so much of your fantasy life, no *actual* dress hanging on a rack will ever live up to your sense of the event's importance. Thirty-two-year-old Shelley spent over three months looking for the ideal dress to wear to the extravagant synagogue wedding and country club reception she and her fiancé were planning. "It began to be a sort of quest," she recalled. "I went to bridal shops, department stores; looked at pattern books; consulted with dressmakers. It took so much time that I began putting off other prewedding errands and decisions. I was *obsessed* with finding the most exquisite dress in creation." Eventually, Shelley had to make a choice about a dress— the wedding was two weeks away and she still hadn't decided on anything. "I was nearly hysterical," she says. "I thought the dress I was buying was horrible, but I had to get something. Later, at the wedding, and looking at the wedding pictures, I could see that the dress I picked out was perfectly lovely. But I guess I poured so much other prewedding tension into that choice that I wasn't going to be happy with anything I picked."

Take a lesson from Shelley and don't let your search for the perfect dress assume the proportions of the quest for the Holy Grail. In the end, a dress is nothing more than a dress, and it is highly unlikely that the "wrong" dress will ruin the wedding. While you want to look and feel beautiful, you should avoid becoming obsessed about the perfect dress, because that dress exists only in your imagination.

Keep in mind that the intensity everyone—you, your fiancé, and both your families—bring to the so-called 'petty' details of the wedding is really an expression of the anxiety that you all are feeling about the changes that the upcoming marriage represents. Change is welcomed with ambivalence by most people, and the response is often to try to control it. All the commotion that surrounds the wedding plans often is really just an attempt at controlling the changes that are taking place.

It is also important to understand that these changes are the result of the marriage, not the wedding. But the wedding—and all its attendant details—can become the perfect symbolic substitution. Instead of dealing with their apprehensions about what the newly married couple will mean to them, your families and even friends may be easily thrown off course by the details of the wedding itself.

This kind of displacement—I would call it obsessional substitution—is something that you and your fiancé may be especially susceptible to as well. Often, the endless obsession over which dress, what flowers, or where the wedding is held are ways of not dealing with the real issues of marriage. You forget that you are about to create a new family, because you are so intently focused on creating a party. Like all obsessive behavior, this one contains an element of avoidance. The person who washes her hands fifty times a day may think she is guarding against contamination. But in fact she is really defending herself against some much deeper anxiety, which she doesn't want to face. In the same way, the woman who is obsessed with finding the right wedding dress or perfect location may be masking more profound anxieties.

In addition, this obsessive focus can be a way of maintaining the early elation that follows a decision to marry. It's a way to holding on to the high—of delaying, or doing away with, the need to come down to earth.

Here is a good analogy: I know a couple who spent a great deal of time and energy preparing for the birth of their baby. They read books, went to natural childbirth classes, attended lectures and seminars. They were more than prepared for the birth, but what they had failed to prepare for was the reality of the baby that came from it. In fact, all the elaborate preparations for the birth were unconsciously meant to keep the reality of having a child at bay. The parallel is, I think, clear enough. If you are experiencing an intense, troubling, and obsessive preoccupation with some (or all) of the details of the wedding, you would do well to stop and ask yourself if there is some other issue that you are avoiding or finding it difficult to face.

◆

□ *A Word to the Wise*

After having grappled with the frustration caused by making all of these prewedding decisions, you and your fiancé are apt to feel emotionally drained. If at all possible, give yourselves a brief breather from all the frenetic activity and emotionally charged decision-making. Agree to spend a day, evening, or if feasible, an entire weekend in which you don't mention the wedding plans once. See a movie, head to an amusement park, go bike riding in the country, have a picnic. You've worked hard emotionally to get to this point and you're entitled to a rest.

8.

JUBILATION:

We Did It!

◆

□ *Getting Clear*

At this point you must be well aware of how arduous the path from the engagement to the wedding really is. You have experienced—and hopefully dealt with—a variety of intense emotions, and resolved the thorniest prewedding problems, leaving your way clear to a jubilant wedding day.

Although you may not be aware of it, you and your fiancé have been involved in "demythologizing" the whole process of planning your wedding—that is to say, examining and dispelling many of the commonly held myths about the planning process. The result will be a much more keenly felt experience of the day to come.

You can—and indeed most likely will—have a wedding day that is crystalline in its happiness and its sense of emotional connectedness.

While you initially might have thought that this process of demythologizing would remove the mystery and romance from the wedding, by now you probably realize you have methodically cleared away the mist of some often-unsettling emotions experienced by brides and grooms who do not examine their feelings as they move along. Because these emotions are so contradictory, many brides and grooms insulate themselves from their feelings and end up experiencing a severe case of what might easily be called the "Wedding Day Blurs." They slip through this most important of days feeling dazed and confused, out of touch with what is happening around them. Again and again, you will hear these all-too-familiar post-wedding words: "I hardly felt anything" or "Everything was a kind of blur" or "I felt like I was in a trance most of the time," and finally, "I'm so glad it's over." What a pity that this potentially ecstatic day was not fully experienced by the most potentially important participants in it!

But you and your fiancé can take pride in your sustained willingness to deal with all your feelings and emotions—both the positive and the negative. You have learned to assert the primacy of your role in the wedding and cleared an emotionally congenial space for yourselves. Congratulations—the best is yet to come!

□ *Stags and Does:*
The Bachelor Party and the Bridal Shower

Although you are almost at the finish line, there is still
one more set of prewedding hurdles that you and your
fiancé may face: the bachelor party and the bridal shower.
While these two ritualized events are not mandatory, they
are nevertheless common and are usually scheduled to
take place shortly before the wedding—just at the time
when your emotional intensity is already at its peak. It is
important to remember that neither you nor your fiancé
are obliged to participate in either of these events; you
can discourage well-meaning friends from planning these
parties if you make your feelings about them perfectly
clear. However, neither of you should make the decision
for the other one: you must let your partner come to his
own decision about this, and he must grant you the same
freedom.

As a liberated, contemporary woman, you may well
find the idea of the bachelor—or stag—party offensive.
And indeed, such parties have had a pretty bad reputation:
too much beer, X-rated films, lots of ribbing about getting
married and about women in general. "I couldn't believe
that Ian was actually going to go through with it!" fumes
thirty-year-old Margo. "When his friends suggested a
bachelor party, I was sure that he would say no. But as
it turned out, he was tickled pink by the idea. And I
thought I knew him!" But before Margo gets carried away
by her anger, it might help her—and you—to look back
to some of the emotions you have already dealt with in

165

this book. You will begin to realize that this intense male bonding, which takes place practically on the eve of the wedding, actually may serve an important psychological function for your fiancé. If at any time he has felt—and indeed it is highly probable he has—that his identity as a man will be compromised by marrying, this concentrated dose of male attention may help assuage those feelings. Don't begrudge him this last gasp of emotional freedom—it doesn't mean he's sexist at heart or that he doesn't deeply love and want to be married to you. Graciously accept his need to get rowdy with his buddies *now* and he may feel less inclined to exercise such prerogatives during your married life.

□ *"Singin' in the Rain"*

Wedding showers may appear to be less emotionally problematic—at least on the surface. Traditionally, the image of the bridal shower has been less overtly sexual (though this is, as will be discussed in a bit, changing) and more benign. Nevertheless, you can still run up against some emotional snags that are worth guarding against, with a little thinking and planning ahead:

• *The Surprise Shower.* While some women may adore the idea of being surprised by close friends and relatives, you may not be one of them. If this is the case, you might want to warn, well in advance, those friends who may be planning such events. Thirty-two-year-old Ginny described her surprise wedding shower this way: "I had just come from a frantic day of prewedding shopping with my mother and fiancé. I couldn't find the right shoes anywhere, and two of the bridesmaid's gifts—monogrammed silver pens—came back with mistakes and had to be done all over again. My fiancé and I had just had a silly argument over something and I was still fuming about it when I opened the door and all these people yelled 'Surprise!' My hair was dirty; I was crabby, tired, upset, and all I wanted to do was crawl into bed with a juicy murder mystery and a pint of double-fudge ice cream. Instead, I had to pretend to be thrilled while I opened three toasters, two popcorn-makers, and an electric juicer that looked complicated enough to blast off into outer space!"

◆ *The Theme Shower*. Even if your wedding shower is not a surprise, you may want to indicate your gift preferences discreetly to the hostess of the party. Otherwise, the hostess—or another guest—may suggest a theme that you find embarrassing or discomforting. For instance, take the bridal shower hostess for twenty-seven-year-old Nora, a high school history teacher. Since she didn't specify a theme or a preferred type of gift, her best friend—and the shower's hostess—told all the guests to bring suggestive lingerie. "I really felt a little awkward opening box after box of see-through nightgowns, sheer teddies, and red satin panties while sitting next to my straight-laced, church-going mother! Needless to say, she gave me a thick terry bathrobe and some flannel pajamas as a shower gift."

◆ *The Sexy Shower*. Although the stag party has the reputation of having an overtly sexual theme, many contemporary women have assumed such prerogatives when planning bridal showers for their friends. Twenty-one-year-old Dina was really looking forward to the shower her close pals were arranging, even though they wouldn't tell her much about what it would entail. She was shocked to find that the highlight of the evening was a male stripper who had been hired to "do his thing" at the party. Even worse, her guests brought "joke" gifts, such as a Frisbee—meant to suggest an oversized diaphragm—accompanied by a large tube of contraceptive cream, a very graphically illustrated marriage manual, and the like. "I know they meant it to be funny," she recalls, "but the whole thing just seemed in bad taste to me. I wish they had asked before they went ahead and planned something like that. I was really embarrassed!"

The moral of these three stories is not so different from the one this book has stressed throughout: If you don't make your feelings and wishes clearly known at all stages of the wedding-planning process, you may well find yourself disappointed, resentful, and downright unhappy. Never forget that you have the primary responsibility for your own happiness, and this is as true for the bridal shower as it is for the most other aspects of your wedding. If you have strong feelings about what you want—or don't want—at your shower, make sure the people in charge are well aware of those feelings.

□ *The Prewedding Jitters*

The day before the wedding has a special place in life's canon of anxiety-producing moments. You and your fiancé may find that you experience—in an encapsulated form—*all* of the emotions that you have been reading about here, in the space of these tense twenty-four hours. As a result, the two of you may find that you're walking on eggs around each other and that you would even like to get away from each other for a little while. This is especially true if you are already living together and sharing an intimate, domestic space.

Relax. Your reaction is so normal that it has even developed a small ritual of its own: Folklore decrees, and many people still believe, that it is bad luck for the bride and groom to see each other right before the wedding. Therefore, you may well want to consider the possibility of *not* spending the night prior to the wedding with each other. Although you may find this archaic—particularly if the two of you have already set up housekeeping together—it has some distinct emotional benefits.

Take the case of Lester and Rita, who had been living together for the last two years. The night before their wedding, Lester's friends wanted to treat him to an elaborate bachelor night on the town—drinks, dinner, and a round of late-night clubs. Rita had no desire to go along, but she didn't want to be at home—alone—glancing at the clock every fifteen minutes and waiting for Lester to walk in the door. "I called up my sister and asked if I could spend the night at her place. So after dinner, I packed a bag and went over there. It was great! We had our own little slumber party—we talked about old times, gave each other manicures, watched a late movie on TV. In the morning, after a peaceful night's sleep, I went home to get ready for my wedding."

Of course, you have to consider your own personal situation carefully before deciding on such a plan. For thirty-four-year-old Marty, who is black, and thirty-year-old Phoebe, who is white, the prewedding period had been an arduous and often painful period of trying to get both families to accept their union. "I was quite scared about how it would all turn out," says Phoebe. "I needed Marty there for moral and even physical support. Forget the tradition—if we had been separated the night before, I would have been in no shape for the wedding." Once again, the lesson is clear: You must tailor the prewedding ritual to suit your own particular needs.

Finally, if you and your fiancé have not slept together, you may find yourself filled with a mixture of desire and nervousness in anticipation of your wedding night. In this case—as with all the others—you should plan to spend the night before the wedding in whatever way makes the two of you feel most comfortable. This may mean a quiet dinner with your fiancé, a lively celebration with members of the wedding party, or an intimate family gathering. Whatever you choose, make sure that is responsive to your emotional state.

☐ *"Oh What a Beautiful Mornin'..."*

You and your fiancé have somehow managed to make it through the night, and the wedding day has finally dawned. To ensure that it starts out on the right foot, consider the following ways of avoiding any unnecessary emotional or practical complications:

● Don't give yourselves *any* chores, tasks, errands, or responsibilities. Having to run errands on the day you are getting married leaves you wide open to last-minute hysteria, which you want to avoid at all costs. So simply decide—in advance—that you won't use the wedding day to pick up a suit, a case of wine, or have your hair cut. Instead, make sure that these details are taken care of before the actual wedding day, by either doing them yourself or enlisting the assistance of family and friends.

● Do give yourselves ample time to dress and arrive where you need to be in advance of the appointed hour. It is amazing how little emergencies—a run in your pantihose, a torn seam or hem—can crop up at the last minute, so make sure you have plenty of time to attend to these or any others that may arise. Give some thought to transportation, too—*don't* wait until the last minute to catch a cab or hop in your car. If necessary, make sure you have maps and careful directions to your destination. Give your car a full tank of gas the day before. You want everything to be smooth sailing, not last-minute rushing.

● Don't bring up any topics that are sensitive or controversial between you and your fiancé. This is most emphatically *not* the time to talk about your fiancé's inability to balance his checkbook, failure to do his share of the housework, or persistent habit of interrupting when you are telling a story.

Although this may sound contradictory, given the preceding chapters—with their focus on confrontation and honest revelation of feelings—you must remember that timing is all-important in any emotional encounter. Neither you nor you fiancé will be in any shape to discuss the nuances of your relationship today, and it is all too easy to pick a fight over some unrelated issue as a way of expressing your own prewedding tension. Be aware of this tendency, and make sure that you weigh your words carefully before you speak. This is a moment to be forgiving and accepting; not one for intense emotional scrutiny.

♦ Do consider the impact of dealing with friends and family before the wedding. If your best girlfriend warms your heart and soothes your soul, by all means see her before the big event. But if you know that your mother's anxiety or your father's perfectionism is going to rub off on you and get you rattled, then it's best not to see them until the wedding is at hand.

□ *A Time to Celebrate*

This is it, the moment you have been awaiting—sometimes eagerly, sometimes anxiously—for months. Your wedding day has finally arrived. And if you have done your emotional homework all along, the day should be a memorable and jubilation-filled one for both of you. But there are still some last-minute questions you should consider in advance of the wedding day to ensure that things continue to go smoothly at the big event itself:

◆ *How much time do you devote to your guests?* The answer to this question may seem obvious, but it's not. Although you clearly want at the very least to make brief contact with each and every person who attends your wedding, you don't want to feel like a professional hostess or neglect your new mate. This is a perfect opportunity for friends and close family members to help out. Enlist their aid beforehand—and chances are they will be delighted that you have asked—in making sure that people are properly introduced, seated, enjoying their food, and generally having a good time. You can mention in advance that you want certain individuals to meet one another, and point them out at the reception to whomever you have asked to assume this responsibility.

If you have invited relatives you haven't seen in a long time and are concerned that you might not recognize them, make sure another family member brings that person over and introduces him or her to you.

Finally, if you are having a large wedding, consider the old-fashioned but eminently useful receiving line; this will ensure that you have performed your social obligation by greeting all of your guests. Once that is done, you are more free to relax and enjoy yourselves without worrying that someone has been slighted or ignored.

◆ *Should you (and/or your fiancé) make a toast?* Traditionally, the bride and groom have been perceived of as the recipients of the wedding, and so it is usually left to other people to do the toasting. But this traditional image may not accurately reflect your situation, especially if you and your groom have paid for all or part of the wedding yourselves. You may want to make your own toast; making a toast is an excellent opportunity to thank friends, family, or whomever, and to share your warm feelings with all present. Toasts have an important emotional significance: They give the event a shape and structure, and tend to be remembered by those who heard them. Since you and your groom have used the entire prewedding period as one of self-discovery and movement toward self-knowledge, the toast you make can be a subtle but important symbol of your emotional progress and the healthy sense of control of your own wedding that you have assumed all along.

◆ *What do we do about relatives and friends who try to steal the show?* In chapters 3 and 4 there are more detailed discussions of family and friends who resist your marriage or unconsciously feel resentful of the attention your wedding will bring to you. Unfortunately, despite all your hard work, these feelings may not be entirely resolved by the wedding day, and you may find that a relative, or even a friend, attempts—unintentionally—to take over the event. This happened to Jennifer and Mark, whose wedding reception was nearly dominated by Mark's father—an amateur musician—who sat down at the piano and started to play. "For the first fifteen minutes or so, it was really quite nice," says Jennifer. "Mark's dad plays well enough and I could see that everyone was enjoying the music. But as fifteen minutes turned into twenty and then thirty, I began to panic. The room was fairly small; the piano music was loud—the guests couldn't talk and I could see people felt awkward about walking in front of the piano to get to the bar. I thought the day was just going to be ruined!" Fortunately, Mark had the presence of mind to turn to his brother—also his best man—and say, "Please do something—fast." Because his brother was less tense about the whole event—after all, it wasn't his wedding—he was able to walk up to his father and say tactfully, 'Thanks for the concert, Dad; it was great!' Mark's father got the message, and the threat of musical domination had been lifted.

◆ *How do you handle a problem drinker?* It is entirely possible—and even likely—that at least one person at your wedding will have too much to drink at the reception. While that is not a problem in and of itself, it can mean trouble if that person becomes too loud, demanding, hostile, or in any other way obnoxious as a result of his or her inebriation. Naturally, you want your guests to have a wonderful time at your wedding, but not at your expense or that of the others who have been invited. When Megan and Elliot got married, Megan's godmother, Jeanne, downed a few too many scotches during the course of the afternoon. Normally a charming and vivacious woman, excessive liquor made her belligerent and quarrelsome, and she began trying to initiate a fight with another one of Megan's relatives with whom she had never gotten along. Megan herself walked over to where the altercation was brewing and managed to divert Jeanne's attention. But the situation went from bad to worse.

"As soon as the wedding cake was brought out, Jeanne went racing over and cut herself a huge piece of it! When the other guests saw her eating the cake, they assumed that it had already been served and they started helping themselves. Elliot and I never got to cut the cake together!" Megan says, disappointment still evident in her tone. "Obviously, that didn't ruin the day, but I was still worried over what she might do next. And by that point I felt too demoralized to go after her again. I didn't know how to handle her." As it turned out, Megan's mother, who had known Jeanne for many years and was familiar with her drinking, had observed the incident with the cake. Without saying anything, she appeared at Jeanne's side with a cup of strong black coffee. After Jeanne had finished the coffee, Megan's mother took her outdoors for "a breath of fresh air." By the time the two returned, the crisis had been averted. Megan's mother kept watch on Jeanne's trips to the bar and any further gaffes were happily avoided.

In all of these situations, your best course of action is essentially the same. This is the moment to really *use* your family and friends—bridesmaids, best man, et al.— to help you through the sticky moments. You and your groom are already the focus of enough attention and responsibility; having to deal with troublesome guests puts an undue emotional burden on your shoulders. For that reason, it is best to designate a few "troubleshooters" before the wedding, precisely to take control of situations that threaten to get out of hand.

□ *The Escape Clause: Elopement*

Let's assume that you have read the preceding chapters with care and experienced the entire gamut of emotions, from elation to frustration. You have seriously deliberated with yourself, and finally, after much soul-searching, you decide that you simply can't go through with planning and participating in a traditional wedding. And yet, you still want to get married. At this point, are you allowed to turn to your beloved and ask, "Can't we just elope?"

The answer is a resoundingly clear yes. Weddings really are not for everyone. There are sometimes situations that are too difficult, or too out of control for you to handle: You simply can't face the undying animosity of your divorced parents; you've just taken a demanding new job and you haven't the emotional wherewithal to plan a wedding; the religious or racial differences between you and your partner are causing turmoil in both your families; you don't presently, nor do you expect to have, the financial resources to make the kind of wedding you both want. In any of these situations—and you might find that you have a combination of two or more of them—elopement may be just the escape clause that you've been looking for.

□ *Beyond Success and Failure*

Elopement need not be considered a failed wedding. To the contrary, eloping is a viable emotional alternative and can be a sign of a healthy kind of psychic self-knowledge, Here are some of the pluses that make eloping a truly positive experience:

◆ You can experience a wedding that is closer to being a private exchange of vows and shared feelings than a traditional wedding with guests will permit.

◆ You can liberate yourselves from the intense time pressure that more traditional weddings create, which is a real boon for those who lead busy lives—there is nothing worse than a wedding that has become an organizational headache rather then an emotional apotheosis.

◆ You will eliminate the financial worry that is attendant upon most traditional weddings.

If the primacy of the wedding is the commitment made between you and your beloved, deciding to elope in no way diminishes the meaning of that vow. Ironically enough, eloping may actually allow you and your fiancé to have precisely the kind of emotional experience you wanted all along. And if you use the same criteria in planning the elopement that you would in planning the wedding—that is, every aspect of the experience should be meaningful to both of you—then you can have an intensely romantic and personal wedding, even without any of the traditional trappings.

This was most certainly the case for twenty-nine-year-old Sharon and her thirty-nine-year-old fiancé, Mitchell. Sharon was a sales and marketing analyst at the same New York City advertising agency where Mitchell was the director of the copywriting department. They were certainly both in a financial position to plan a good-sized wedding. And since they had met—and been warmly accepted—by each other's families, there was no problem on that score either. But both Sharon and Mitchell had been married before, and each had gone through a lengthy and elaborate planning process the first time around. While they were very sure of their feelings for one another, neither one had any desire to go through that kind of involved wedding planning again. Elopement seemed like a perfectly reasonable and attractive option. And according to Sharon, it turned out to be even better than that. "Mitch and I decided that getting married was going to be an absolute secret—we told no one we were planning to do it, not even our parents and certainly not any of our friends or colleagues. One sunny Tuesday morning, we both called in sick. Then we got dressed—Mitch was wearing a new navy linen suit and I had on a beautiful pink silk dress—and headed out to our favorite coffee shop for eggs and toast. Dominick, the short-order cook, noticed we were strolling in at 10:30 instead of our usual 8:15 and even asked if we had both been fired or something, but we just smiled into our coffee and said nothing. Then we caught a cab down to City Hall. While we were waiting in line—in New York, you wait for everything—we met this really nice couple, and we agreed to be witnesses for each other. Then, almost before we knew it, it was our turn and we were in the chapel and getting married! The ceremony was short and sweet, and suddenly my new husband was squeezing my hand and kissing me. After the wedding, we found another cab and headed uptown to the Four Seasons restaurant where we ate a wonderful lunch. Then we wandered over to Tiffany's on Fifth Avenue to buy ourselves wedding gifts, since we knew we weren't going to get them from most people. We bought two sterling silver place settings and two exquisite champagne glasses. Then at around 4:30, we headed over to our office, which wasn't far away, and announced to everyone we had just gotten married! All of our friends at work insisted on taking us out to dinner, and we had a terrific time laughing and making toasts like crazy. Then Mitchell and I went back to the Waldorf-Astoria, where he had reserved a room. Alone at last, we had a quiet late supper with plenty of champagne that room service brought up to us. And the next morning, over breakfast—caviar and sour cream omelettes washed down by more champagne—we called our families and told them the news. I think we had the most wonderful wedding in the world!"

For Sharon and Mitchell, eloping was clearly a joyful experience commensurate with their feelings for each other. But if what you really want is a wedding that gathers friends and family together; a special and memorable day that is shared with the ones you love, then eloping may well create a sense of disappointment, loss, and a feeling of being cheated. Eloping should not make you feel that you are denying yourselves something; if it does, then it is not the right choice for you.

□ *An Emotional Safety Valve*

Whether or not eloping is in fact the best thing for you and your fiancé to do, there is much to be gained emotionally simply by discussing the possibility of doing it. In fact, thinking about eloping may turn out to be the all-important way to get *back* on track and regain your equanimity. As this book has stressed all along, taking the time to verbalize your fantasies, state your fears, and explore all the alternatives in a given situation provides an enormous sense of emotional liberation and often relief.

For some couples, planning an elopement may actually confirm the decision to have a traditional wedding. This was certainly the case for thirty-two-year-old Rose and thirty-one-year-old Aaron. A number of converging emotional pressures had made them decide against having a traditional wedding: Rose's five-year-old daughter from a previous marriage was undergoing a particularly difficult period emotionally and she hadn't yet accepted the idea of her new stepfather; Aaron's mother was very ill and frequently hospitalized; Rose had just started her own Boston-based catering business with a partner and all her available cash had been sunk into it; Aaron's Jewish parents hadn't yet grown accustomed to the idea of his marrying a Catholic woman. All in all, it seemed like an inauspicious time to plan a wedding.

"At first, I was kind of excited by the idea of eloping,"

said Rose. "I bought a book of Massachusetts country inns and started looking for a place we could drive to and get married. We planned to leave my daughter with my parents and make a long, three-day weekend of it. The whole thing sounded very romantic and special, and I was really looking forward to it."

What happened to change Rose and Aaron's mind? "I rented the car, made the reservation at the inn, and arranged for my business partner to take care of the business herself for those few days," remembers Rose, "but when I told Aaron that the plans had been made, his face fell. 'What's wrong?' I asked, and he told me. Aaron felt— and as he described his feelings I began to see his point— that what we were planning was wrong because it had no real emotional meaning for us. 'We are going to drive to a strange place where no one knows us and we know no one and get married. I just feel too cut off.' "

The more they discussed it, the more they agreed: Despite all the problems, they wanted a wedding. "Your daughter should be there," Aaron said to Rose, "and so should my parents. We all have to learn to love one another, not to run away."

And so, without intending it, Rose and Aaron planned a wedding. They went through their rough times, to be sure, and at moments they regretted their decision and were sorry they hadn't stuck to their original plan. But they confronted each obstacle one at a time, and were gradually able to make headway. Aaron started spending a lot of time with Rose's daughter, and slowly she began to like, and feel comfortable, with him. Rose went through a similar campaign with Aaron's mother and father. The wedding was to take place at Aaron's parents' home in Cambridge—a plan that would save the couple money and spare Aaron's mother any traveling. A judge who was a friend of Aaron's parents agreed to perform the ceremony. And although their money was indeed limited, they were able to afford a modest gathering of family and friends. Rose's partner in the catering business made her gift the lovely catered meal that was served, and Rose's mother, happy that her daughter was getting married again, offered to make Rose a wedding dress. When the wedding day rolled around, Rose and Aaron were jubilant. They had met the challenges and overcome them; for Rose and Aaron, the wedding day was filled with all the emotional meaning and jubilation they could have hoped for.

After the weeks or perhaps months of struggle, conflict, and problem-solving that have gone on, you and your fiancé can feel justifiably proud of the hard work you've done and all the progress that you have made. The jubilation you're feeling at this moment is truly earned—based on mature recognition and understanding of yourself and your partner. More than simply a promise, the wedding vows the two of you are about to take have already been demonstrated in the actual commitment you have shown to one another during this period.

Since I believe that what happens during the engagement period often serves as a model for what will

183

happen in the marriage that follows, your willingness to work on your difficulties now, before the marriage, is a highly positive indicator for the future of your relationship.

◆

☐ *A Fond Farewell*

No matter what your situation, you and your fiancé can make your wedding day into one of the happiest days of your lives. For some couples, that will mean a gala affair of 350 people; for others, it will be a completely private exchange of vows. But whatever you decide to do, if you do it out of a deep sense of your own volition and desire—and not to fulfill the expectations others have of you—you and your beloved can feel the wondrous power of having created your own happiness and a wedding that is filled with enough joyous memories to face whatever your future together will bring.

FOR THE BEST IN PAPERBACKS, LOOK FOR THE

In every corner of the world, on every subject under the sun, Penguin represents quality and variety—the very best in publishing today.

For complete information about books available from Penguin—including Pelicans, Puffins, Peregrines, and Penguin Classics—and how to order them, write to us at the appropriate address below. Please note that for copyright reasons the selection of books varies from country to country.

In the United Kingdom: For a complete list of books available from Penguin in the U.K., please write to *Dept E.P., Penguin Books Ltd, Harmondsworth, Middlesex, UB7 0DA.*

In the United States: For a complete list of books available from Penguin in the U.S., please write to *Dept BA, Penguin*, Box 120, Bergenfield, New Jersey 07621-0120.

In Canada: For a complete list of books available from Penguin in Canada, please write to *Penguin Books Ltd, 2801 John Street, Markham, Ontario L3R 1B4.*

In Australia: For a complete list of books available from Penguin in Australia, please write to the *Marketing Department, Penguin Books Ltd, P.O. Box 257, Ringwood, Victoria 3134.*

In New Zealand: For a complete list of books available from Penguin in New Zealand, please write to the *Marketing Department, Penguin Books (NZ) Ltd, Private Bag, Takapuna, Auckland 9.*

In India: For a complete list of books available from Penguin, please write to *Penguin Overseas Ltd, 706 Eros Apartments, 56 Nehru Place, New Delhi, 110019.*

In Holland: For a complete list of books available from Penguin in Holland, please write to *Penguin Books Nederland B.V., Postbus 195, NL-1380AD Weesp, Netherlands.*

In Germany: For a complete list of books available from Penguin, please write to *Penguin Books Ltd, Friedrichstrasse 10-12, D-6000 Frankfurt Main I, Federal Republic of Germany.*

In Spain: For a complete list of books available from Penguin in Spain, please write to *Longman, Penguin España, Calle San Nicolas 15, E-28013 Madrid, Spain.*

In Japan: For a complete list of books available from Penguin in Japan, please write to *Longman Penguin Japan Co Ltd, Yamaguchi Building, 2-12-9 Kanda Jimbocho, Chiyoda-Ku, Tokyo 101, Japan.*

2944